My Sister in
this House

by Wendy Kesselman

A tape of the music and sound effects of the play is available from
Gary and Timmy Harris, 533 West 121st Street, New York, NY 10027.

D0111353

A SAMUEL FRENCH ACTING EDITION

SAMUEL FRENCH
FOUNDED 1830

New York Hollywood London Toronto

SAMUELFRENCH.COM

ACTORS THEATRE OF LOUISVILLE
THE STATE THEATRE OF KENTUCKY

JON JORY, *Producing-Director*

Presents

with the generous assistance of HUMANA INC.

February 18 through March 29, 1981

The Fifth Annual
Festival of New American Plays

My Sister
In This House

by WENDY KESSELMAN

Directed by	JON JORY
Set Design	PAUL OWEN
Costume Design	KURT WILHELM
Lighting Design	PAUL OWEN
Sound Design	JOHN NORTH
Co-Property Masters	SAM GARST
	SANDRA STRAWN
Stage Manager	TOM ABERGER
Assistant Stage Manager	RICHARD A. CUNNINGHAM

First produced by Actors Theatre of Louisville.

Cast of Characters

Christine	CRISTINE ROSE
Lea	PATRICIA CHARBONNEAU
Madame Cottin	ELOISE TERRY
Mademoiselle Isabelle Danzard	MARIANNE OWEN
Madame Danzard	ANNE PITONIAK
Photographer	ANDY BACKER

The recorded voices are KEN JENKINS as the "Chief Justice,"
TOM McPAUL as the "Priest," MICHAEL KEVIN as the "Judge,"
and DAVID JAFFE as the "Policeman."

There will be one intermission this evening.

Place: Le Mans, France
Time: The play takes place during the years 1925 through 1933
in different houses in and around the town of Le Mans.

Presented by special arrangement with the Lucy Kroll Agency.

3

THE SECOND STAGE

A Non-Profit Theatre Oganization

Robyn Goodman & Carole Rothman
Artistic Directors

presents

MY SISTER IN THIS HOUSE

by WENDY KESSELMAN

Directed by
INVERNA LOCKPEZ & CAROLE ROTHMAN

Starring

LISA BANES   **BEVERLY MAY**
BRENDA CURRIN   **ELIZABETH McGOVERN**

Set Design   *Lighting Design*   *Costume Design*
JIM CLAYBURGH   **ARDEN FINGERHUT**   **SUSAN HILFERTY**

Sound Design   *Production Stage Manager*
GARY HARRIS   **FREDRIC H. ORNER**

Hair Design   *Stage Manager*
ANTONIO SODDU   **JUDITH ANN CHEW**

Production Supervisor for The Second Stage: KIM NOVICK

CASTING BY SIMON AND KUMIN
MEG SIMON and FRAN KUMIN

New York City production by The Second Stage.

First produced by Actors Theatre Of Louisville.

This production is made possible in part with public funds from the New York State Council on the Arts.

CAST
(in order of appearance)

CHRISTINE .... *Lisa Banes*
LEA .... *Elizabeth McGovern*
MADAME DANZARD .... *Beverly May*
ISABELLE....................................... *Brenda Currin*

The play takes place in Le Mans, France during the early 1930's. It is based on an historical incident which occurred in Le Mans in 1933.

"My Sister In This House" is performed without an intermission.

"My Sister In This House" was the recipient of the 1980 Susan Smith Blackburn Award.

"My Sister In This House" received the 1980 Playbill Award, given annually by New Dramatists to the year's most promising script.

"My Sister In This House" is a professional production employing
members of Actors Equity Assn. The Second Stage is a member
of the Off Off Broadway Alliance.

PRODUCTION STAFF

Assistant Stage Manager .... Ami Rothschild
Assistant Set Design .... Bill Motyka
Assistant Costume Design .... Eileen Miller
Properties...................................... Laura Toffler
Technical Director .... Louis Berman
Wardrobe...................................... Eileen Miller
Carpenters........................ Charles Owen, Tommy Louie

STAFF FOR THE SECOND STAGE

Associate Director............................... Drew Farber
Press Consultant .... Richard Kornberg
Theatre Manager .... Lindy Rollo
Attorney............. Paul, Weiss, Rifkind, Wharton and Garrison;
      Michael Kaufman, John Silberman, John Breglio
      and Fred Heather
Management Firm .... Pentacle Management;
      Mara Greenberg, Ivan Sygoda
House Manager .... Ray Blake
Box Office Manager.......................... Meredith January
Graphic Design............................... Deborah Peretz
Photographer.................................. Stephanie Saia
Interns....................... Sarah Golden, Meredith January,
      Kathy Kosmidor, Laura Toffler, Michael Zam
Literary Assistants .... Allison Burnett, Alice Dewey,
      Robert Alan Gerber
House Physician .... Stuart Forster, M.D.

5

CHARACTERS

CHRISTINE

LEA,* her sister

MADAME DANZARD

ISABELLE, her daughter

VOICE OF PHOTOGRAPHER

VOICE OF MEDICAL EXAMINER

VOICE OF JUDGE

PLACE: Le Mans, France

TIME: The play takes place during the early 1930's. It is based on an historical incident which occurred in Le Mans in 1933.

*Pronounced Léa

My Sister In This House

ACT ONE

SCENE 1

CHRISTINE. (*Voice over.*) (*Sings.*)
Sleep my little sister, sleep
Sleep through darkness
Sleep so deep

Lights comes up slowly on the faces of CHRISTINE *and* LEA
as if framed in a photograph.

CHRISTINE. (*Continued.*)
All the rivers find the sea
My little sister
Sleep for me.

Dream my little sister, dream
Dream I'm here now
Dream your dreams
All the things you want to be
My little sister
Dream for me.*

(CHRISTINE *and* LEA *stand side by side at the edge of the stage.* CHRISTINE *wears a faded dress with a white apron,* LEA. *a simple childlike dress.* CHRISTINE'S *hair is wound either in two buns, one on each side of her face, or in braids circling her head.* LEA'S *hair hangs in a long braid.*

*Copyright © 1981 of "Sleep My Little Sister, Sleep"
Lyrics and Music by Wendy Kesselman
See p. 82 for music.

See p. 82 for music.

7

CHRISTINE *is just twenty*, LEA, *still an adolescent.* LEA *gazes vaguely into the distance.* CHRISTINE *looks straight ahead. They move apart.* CHRISTINE *begins polishing a brass candlestick.* LEA *looks out.*)

LEA. Dear Christine. When Maman left me here on Friday, I thought I would die. They didn't want to take me at first, but Maman told Madame Crespelle I was fifteen. Christine, I wish you could see what they eat. You can't imagine the desserts. The cook told me Madame's favorite dish is duck with cherries and Monsieur's, chicken with champagne. I'm hungry all the time. But it isn't as bad as I expected. I even have my own room. Do you think you could ask Madame Roussel to change your day off to Wednesday, like mine? (*She pauses.*) Today Madame Crespelle smiled at me. She was pleased with how the silver looked. I had been polishing it all morning. It was worth every minute for Madame's smile. When she smiles she looks just like Sister Veronica. (*A bell rings.* LEA *moves closer to* CHRISTINE.) Three days ago Maman came and took me away. She said I could earn more money somewhere else. I was just getting used to the Crespelles, but I'm getting four more francs a month and Maman's promised to let me keep one of them. The Cottins have one daughter, Mademoiselle Sophie. Her birthday is next week. She's only two months older than me. She's so pretty. Her skin is like milk. And Christine, you should hear her play the piano. (*She pauses.*) Madame Cottin counts everything. Even the chocolates in the glass bowl. But I remember everything you taught me. And I think Madame will be pleased with me. (*She pauses.*) Every morning Madame Cottin examines my fingernails before I make the beds. Her things are so delicate. So many ruffles. So many buttons. You wouldn't believe how many buttons. It takes me two hours to iron one dress. And even then Madame isn't satisfied. (*She pauses.*) In this house I'm always afraid I'll do something wrong. Not like you, Christine. You never make mistakes *(She pauses. Longingly.)* Oh Christine, if only Maman would place us together. (*A bell rings, almost interrupting* LEA'S *last sentence.* LEA *goes down on her hands and knees and begins polishing the floor.* CHRISTINE *looks out.*)

CHRISTINE. (*Tender.*) Don't worry, Lea. You don't have to worry. It's only a matter of time. Just time before you get used to it. (*She pauses.*) Don't worry what they say to you. (*She pauses.*) I mean . . . don't take it to heart. I know that's hard in the beginning. But you'll learn. It's just time. (*She pauses.*) You'll see. Remember what Maman says—"When you've worked for them as long as I have—then you'll see." (*She pauses.*) Some are better than others, Lea. Believe me. You just never know. (*She pauses.*) Don't worry about writing every day. I know how tired you must be. But don't hide anything from me. And if—if they make you cry—I want you to let me know right away. (*A bell rings. Light comes up on the interior of the* DANZARD *house in Le Mans, France. A combined dining room and sitting room is divided from the kitchen by a narrow staircase going up to a landing, and continuing to a maid's room. The house can also be created in a less realistic way. However, the staircase is an intrinsic element of the structure of the set.*)

CHRISTINE *and* LEA *pick up shabby suitcases. They smile at each other. They go upstairs to the maid's room. The room is shabby, small. There is a single bed, a night table, a sink and a mirror. There is a small skylight.* LEA *opens the door and rushes into the room.* CHRISTINE *follows her.*

LEA.(*Excited.*) I can't believe it. I just can't believe it. (*She puts her suitcase down on the floor.*) How did you do it? How did you get Maman to agree? Tell me.

CHRISTINE. Shhh. They'll hear you downstairs.

LEA. Tell me. You're always keeping something from me. (CHRISTINE *turns away.*) Tell me.

CHRISTINE. (*Turning back, smiling.*) I told her there'd be more money for her this way.

LEA. You're so clever, so smart.

CHRISTINE. I said that till you learned, you had to have someone to protect you.

LEA. And that was you. That was you. Am I right, Christine? (*She reaches to hug* CHRISTINE.)

CHRISTINE. (*Shivering.*) The room's cold. (*She lifts her suitcase onto the bed.*)

LEA. Remember what you used to call me? My feet still get cold at night. They get like ice. (CHRISTINE *opens her suitcase, starts putting her things away. She has few belongings.*)

CHRISTINE. (*Smiling.*) Come on. Put your suitcase up here with mine. I'll unpack it for you. (*She picks up* LEA'S *suitcase and puts it on the bed. She begins to unpack it for* LEA.)

LEA. Now they'll be warm. (CHRISTINE *takes a small crocheted blanket out of* LEA's *suitcase.*)

CHRISTINE. What — you still have this old thing?

LEA. I had to take it. She was with me when I packed.

CHRISTINE. (*Turning away.*) Well, I don't care. It has nothing to do with me.

LEA. Don't you like it?

CHRISTINE. It's old and falling apart. I never liked Maman's sewing. It's vulgar. (*Silently, she continues unpacking their things.*)

LEA. (*Watching her.*) What's the matter? Aren't you

glad that we're together?

CHRISTINE. Why didn't you take the other room? They offered it to you.

LEA. But I wanted to be with you.

CHRISTINE. The other room was nice. Nicer than this one.

LEA. Christine? (CHRISTINE *is silent.*) I don't understand. You worked the whole thing out and now you don't even want me with you.

CHRISTINE. Of course I want you with me.

LEA. What's wrong then?

CHRISTINE. Nothing's wrong. (*There is a pause.*)

LEA. I'll throw the blanket away if you want. I don't care about it. I just want you to be happy.

CHRISTINE. (*Finally turning around.*) But I am happy, little cold feet. (*She takes the blanket from* LEA.) We'll put the blanket right here. (*She lays the blanket at the foot of the bed.*) The main thing is that now we are together. (*Slowly the light on* CHRISTINE *and* LEA *dims. Light has begun to come up on* MADAME DANZARD *and* MADEMOISELLE ISABELLE DANZARD *downstairs in the sitting room.* MADAME DANZARD *is polishing* ISABELLE'S *nails.* MADAME DANZARD *is in her early fifties,* ISABELLE *in her early twenties, the same age as* CHRISTINE.)

MADAME DANZARD. This pink is lovely on you. So much better than the clear. Clear, clear, clear. It seems to be all everyone's wearing. This is such a bright color.

ISABELLE. You don't think it's too bright, do you, Maman? Do you think it's too bright?

MADAME DANZARD. Too bright? Nonsense. Bright colors are coming back. Hold still. This is delicate work, my dear. Highly delicate. This has to be perfect. (*She finishes the last nail of* ISABELLE'S *left hand.*) There! Now the other one. (ISABELLE *examines her hand.*) I'm waiting. (ISABELLE *holds out her other hand.*) So my dear, what do you think?

ISABELLE. About what, Maman?

MADAME DANZARD. What do you mean—about what, Maman? About them. About what else?

ISABELLE. Oh . . . they seem fine.

MADAME DANZARD. Fine? Is that all you can say? As a matter of fact, I think we may be in for a pleasant surprise.

ISABELLE. If you say so, Maman.

MADAME DANZARD. (*After a pause.*) Can't you at least express an opinion? You know how I value your opinion, Isabelle.

ISABELLE. Yes Maman. I know.

MADAME DANZARD. I wouldn't have taken the younger one. It's always a risk. But seeing that she's in the family. (*Putting the nail brush in the bottle and shaking it vigorously.*) Sisters! What could be better? And two almost for the price of one. We'll save on everything. They didn't even want two rooms. (*Carefully touching up one nail.*) Just this little corner. Apparently the older one sews extraordinarily well. She's your age, you know. "Such embroidery, such needlework," they said. I've never seen recommendations like that from Saint Mary of the Fields.

ISABELLE. Sewing. That's all they ever teach them.

MADAME DANZARD. Well, it's all to the good. If there're any alterations on your new dress she'll make them. We won't even have to go to the dressmaker's.

ISABELLE. What luck.

MADAME DANZARD. I remember our neighbor Monsieur Blanqui hiding one of those convent girls. I saw her once from my window. She must have been just my age. She looked a little like the older sister. She'd run away from the convent.

ISABELLE. Run away. Really?

MADAME DANZARD. Every now and then one got away. I never understood how she escaped. That wall! There was not one place you could see inside. I used to hear her at night begging them not to send her back. "Not there. Not to that place." In the end even Madame Blanqui didn't want to give her up. Can you imagine—in this town? And believe me they came looking for her.

ISABELLE. They did, Maman?

MADAME DANZARD. They used to comb each house for those girls. (*She lifts up* ISABELLE'S *hands.*) Look, my dear. Aren't they beautiful? How do you like my handiwork? (*The light fades.*)

SCENE 2

Early morning. CHRISTINE *and* LEA'S *room is almost dark. They are asleep. The alarm clock rings.* CHRISTINE *turns it off. She reaches out to touch* LEA, *curled up beside her. Gently she touches her shoulder, strokes her hair.*

LEA. (*Turning toward* CHRISTINE.) Is it time?

CHRISTINE. Sleep, turtle. Go back in your shell.

LEA. But—

CHRISTINE. Sleep. There's time. I'll wake you. (LEA *turns over again. She is holding the small blanket their Mother has made.* CHRISTINE *covers* LEA'S *shoulder with the blanket. Shivering, she gets out of bed, stands on the cold floor. She puts on her shoes.*) Lea...it's almost six.

LEA. Mmmm. Another minute, Christine. Just one more.

CHRISTINE. Just one—all right. (*At the sink, she washes her face and hands. She shivers from the cold water, fixes her hair in the mirror. She removes her long*

*white nightgown and puts on her maid's uniform. She
goes over to the bed. Tickling* LEA'S *feet.*) Come on now.
Come on. (*She pulls the blanket off* LEA.)

LEA. (*Sitting up.*) It's freezing here. Is it always like
this?

CHRISTINE. (*Laying out* LEA's *uniform on the bed.*)
Always.

LEA. Everywhere you've been?

CHRISTINE. Everywhere.

LEA. (*Putting on her shoes.*) I polished the banister
yesterday. Did you notice how it shines?

CHRISTINE. I noticed. (*To herself.*) I thought it would
be easier with two of us.

LEA. You're disappointed, aren't you? You're unhap-
py with me here. Tell me.

CHRISTINE. Don't be silly.

LEA. I can't seem to do anything right. I can't seem to
please you.

CHRISTINE. You please me, turtle. You please me
more than anything.

LEA. You're so quick. You get things done in a minute.

CHRISTINE. You're fine the way you are.

LEA. (*Struggling with her nightgown.*) Maybe this
was a mistake. I slow you down.

CHRISTINE. Stop it, Lea.

LEA. (*Still struggling.*) Sister Veronica always said I was
too slow. She said I'd never be as quick as you.

CHRISTINE. What did she know?

LEA. You used to think she knew everything.

CHRISTINE. (*Helping* LEA *take off her nightgown.*)
That was a long time ago. I've gotten over all that now.

LEA. You were famous at the convent. Your sewing!
They still have that dress you made for the Virgin Mary.
She's still wearing it.

CHRISTINE. And yet I remember, when I was at Saint

Mary's, I could never go down the stairs like the others. One, two, one, two. I could never take a step with my left foot. It was always my right, my right, my right. I used to envy them running down the stairs when it took me forever.

LEA. Tell me a story, Christine. Just one — before we go down.

CHRISTINE. Which one?

LEA. When I was little

CHRISTINE. You're still little.

LEA. No, I mean really little — you know — the story with the horse.

CHRISTINE. Again? Don't you ever get tired of it.

LEA. No — tell me.

CHRISTINE. (*Making the bed.*) When you were just a tiny thing, Maman sent me out one day to get bread. You came with me, the way you always did. And as we were walking, you let go of my hand and ran into the street to pick something up.

LEA. Tell it slower. You're telling it too fast.

CHRISTINE. It was a *long* narrow street — you remember — on a hill. At the top of the street a horse and carriage loaded with bottles was coming down and galloping right toward you. I ran into the street and pulled you across and pushed you down into the gutter with me. (*Falling down on the bed with* LEA.) What a noise when the horse galloped by! Everyone was screaming. Maman said the horse had gone mad. And when we stood up, we were both bleeding. But it was the same wound. It started on my arm and went down across your wrist. Look—(*She lines up her arm with* LEA's.) We have it still.

LEA. And Maman — what did she say?

CHRISTINE. Oh Maman. Maman was terrified. You know how her face gets. She screamed at us.

LEA. And then — then what happened?

CHRISTINE. Then there was the gypsy—Mad Flower they used to call her.

LEA. And what did she say?

CHRISTINE. She said—oh you—you know it so well.

LEA. But tell me again, Christine. Tell me again.

CHRISTINE. They're bound for life, Mad Flower said. Bound in blood. (*A bell rings.*)

SCENE 3

In this scene the dining room and kitchen are seen simultaneously. MADAME DANZARD *and* ISABELLE *are sitting at the dining room table, finishing the first course of lunch.* CHRISTINE *and* LEA *come into the kitchen. They are wearing their uniforms:* CHRISTINE, *the long severe cook's apron,* LEA, *the delicate serving apron.*

MADAME DANZARD. Don't toy with your food, Isabelle. It's so disagreeable. Always making those little piles.

ISABELLE. I'm not, Maman.

MADAME DANZARD. You mean to tell me I don't see what you're doing.

ISABELLE. I'm not toying, Maman.

MADAME DANZARD. (*Coldly.*) Very well, my dear, call it what you will. (*She rings a small round bell.* LEA *and* CHRISTINE *come into the dining room.* MADAME DANZARD *looks them over carefully.* LEA *is carrying a platter of veal on a tray. She presents the platter for* MADAME DANZARD'S *inspection, as* CHRISTINE *stands to the side.* MADAME DANZARD *smiles to herself.* LEA *puts the platter down and she and* CHRISTINE *go back into the kitchen.* MADAME DANZARD *and* ISABELLE *serve themselves and eat in silence for a few moments.*)

CHRISTINE. (*Following* LEA *into the kitchen.*) She liked it. Did you see? Did you see her face?

LEA. She likes everything you do.

CHRISTINE. She sees everything. (*She sits down at the kitchen table and begins to prepare string beans. Everything* CHRISTINE *does in the kitchen is neat, quick, impeccable. The bowls and plates seem to move like magic beneath her fingers.* LEA *is clearly a beginner. She sits down beside* CHRISTINE *and begins, clumsily, to help her with the beans.*)

MADAME DANZARD. (*Savouring the veal.*) This veal is delicious.

ISABELLE. Of course, you love veal. (*She looks at her mother.*)

MADAME DANZARD. Don't you?

ISABELLE. You know I don't. It's too heavy in the middle of the day.

MADAME DANZARD. Not the way she's prepared it. Light as a feather.

ISABELLE. I've heard it ruins the complexion.

MADAME DANZARD. Where did you hear that?

ISABELLE. I read it.

MADAME DANZARD. (*Scornfully.*) Really. Where?

ISABELLE. Somewhere. I don't remember.

MADAME DANZARD. Certain days of the month, my dear, you really are worse than others.

ISABELLE. That shouldn't surprise *you.*

MADAME DANZARD. Isabelle, if you continue in this vein you're going to ruin my meal. (*She eats with a certain relish.*) Wait till the Blanchards come to dinner. I'll have her make her rabbit paté. Won't that surprise them! The best cook we've had in years.

ISABELLE. Oh I don't know — Marie wasn't so bad.

MADAME DANZARD. Marie? Please. The way she

cooked a pot au feu — ahhh — It still makes me shudder.

ISABELLE. You exaggerate, Maman.

MADAME DANZARD. Exaggerate? I'm being kind. Marie would have murdered a veal like this. (*Wiping her mouth with her napkin.*) Done to perfection. I hope we never lose her. And she always buys the best.

ISABELLE. I don't know how she does it with the money you give her.

MADAME DANZARD. It's what I've always given them. You have no idea how lucky we are, Isabelle. The servants I've seen in my day. (*She watches* ISABELLE *stuff potatoes into her mouth.*) They eat like birds. (*Looking at* ISABELLE.) Always looking so neat, so perfect. You wouldn't think they were maids at all. Though I must admit the younger one gives me trouble — she's so young.

ISABELLE. I like the younger one.

MADAME DANZARD. Well she's quiet. I'll say that for her.

ISABELLE. (*Mercilessly chewing on the veal.*) Quiet? She never speaks. Neither of them do.

MADAME DANZARD. I suppose they must talk between themselves.

ISABELLE. I can't imagine about what.

MADAME DANZARD. (*Looking at* ISABELLE.) Well, maybe they pray. (*She laughs.*) That's how it is when you're brought up by the nuns. (*They both laugh. Abruptly stopping the laughter.*) Will you stop it, Isabelle. Look at that plate. (*She rings the small round bell.* LEA *comes into the dining room with a platter of cheese.* MADAME DANZARD *and* ISABELLE *are instantly silent.* LEA *clears away the empty platter of veal and goes back into the kitchen.*) They're so discreet. Not the slightest prying. You can't imagine what it's like to have a prying maid. To have someone going through your things.

ISABELLE. The younger one washes my things so perfectly. And you know, she's almost pretty.

MADAME DANZARD. (*Cleaning her teeth with her tongue.*) When your father and I were first married — she was something that one. But these two are different. Mark my words.

CHRISTINE. (*Rapidly snapping off the ends of the beans.*) How lucky we are, Lea. The other houses I've been — they come into the kitchen and interfere. Madame knows her place.

MADAME DANZARD. I never even have to tell them anything.

CHRISTINE. I know what she wants before she says a word.

MADAME DANZARD. They take such pride in the house. Not a speck of dust under the carpet.

CHRISTINE. Madame checks everything. I like that.

LEA. You do? It scares me — the way she checks.

MADAME DANZARD. Not a speck.

CHRISTINE. Oh no, I like it. It's better that way. Believe me. In the end it's better.

MADAME DANZARD. Not under the lamps. Not a ring.

ISABELLE. Really?

MADAME DANZARD. Not one. They're extraordinarily clean.

CHRISTINE. Madame is so precise, so careful. Her lists! Everything down to the last second.

LEA. She doesn't let us get away with a thing.

ISABELLE. Well Maman, let's face it — you don't let them get away with a thing.

MADAME DANZARD. Why should I? I pay them enough.

CHRISTINE. Why should she? She wants the house a

certain way.

MADAME DANZARD. This is my house.

ISABELLE. It certainly is.

MADAME DANZARD. Well, it will be yours one day, Isabelle.

CHRISTINE. But she always sees the little things we do.

MADAME DANZARD. The younger one may be pretty, but it's the older one who fascinates me. I've never had anyone like her.

CHRISTINE. I've never had anyone like Madame before.

MADAME DANZARD. Totally trustworthy. I never have to count the change when she comes back from marketing. Not one sou is missing.

CHRISTINE. (*Holding out her bowl to* LEA.) Put them all in here, Lea.

ISABELLE. They don't seem to have any friends.

MADAME DANZARD. Thank heaven for that. (LEA *spills the beans on the floor. She gasps.*)

CHRISTINE. You're so clumsy. (*She begins picking up the beans. Upset,* LEA *helps her.*)

MADAME DANZARD. I've seen those people's friends, my dear. Believe me — it's bad enough with that mother of theirs.

ISABELLE. What a horror! It's a lucky thing they have each other.

CHRISTINE. I didn't mean it. You're so silly. What a baby you are.

MADAME DANZARD. And they do love us. They're so devoted to us. You'll see — the whole town will envy us. (*Laughing.*) We have pearls on our hands, Isabelle. Two pearls. (*They clink their wine glasses.* MADAME DANZARD *rings the small round bell.* ISABELLE *goes over to the sitting room area and takes an evening bag with tiny seed pearls out of a sewing basket.* LEA *and* CHRISTINE *come into the dining room and begin to clear away the dishes.* MADAME DANZARD *goes over to the sewing basket and takes out her needlepoint.*) Let me see, Isabelle. (ISABELLE *holds out the evening bag.*) I can't see it from here. (ISABELLE *leans closer and hands her the bag.* CHRISTINE *and* LEA *work silently together in the kitchen.*) Nice, Very nice. It's coming along. Bit by bit. (*She hands it back to* ISABELLE, *sits down on the couch and begins doing needlepoint.*) You can't rush these things, my dear. Believe me. A bag like that could take you ...(*She looks at* ISABELLE *labouring with the seed pearls.*) Two years. (ISABELLE *looks at her.*) Maybe more. But there's no hurry, is there? Nothing to hurry for. You have all the time in the world.

ISABELLE. Yes Maman.

MADAME DANZARD. All the time. When I was your age I made a bag just like that. Seed pearls too — but mine had a blue background. And when I held it up to the light, it . . .

ISABELLE. It what?

MADAME DANZARD. Shone . . . like little moons. Night after night I worked on that bag. But in the end it was worth it.

ISABELLE. Why, Maman?

MADAME DANZARD. I don't remember. An evening out. A dance.

ISABELLE. Oh what happened, Maman? Tell me.

MADAME DANZARD. I don't know. Maybe nothing. Maybe nothing *ever* happened. Listen to that rain. It's been raining like that for a week. A full week. Who knows when it will stop. Do you hear it, Isabelle?

ISABELLE. I hear it.

MADAME DANZARD. It could go on like this for a

month. That's all we need. Are you listening to me, Isabelle?

ISABELLE. I'm listening, Maman.

MADAME DANZARD. Last year it went on for three months. Remember?

ISABELLE. That was the year before.

MADAME DANZARD. Was it? Was it really. Well, in Paris it's no better. After all, they're further north.

ISABELLE. Do you really think it rains more in Paris than here?

MADAME DANZARD. More, Isabelle. Much more. I'm sure of it. (*After a pause.*) Maybe we'll go up to Paris this year.

ISABELLE. Oh Maman, could we?

MADAME DANZARD. For a little shopping.

ISABELLE. Oh Maman. When?

MADAME DANZARD. Though I don't know. The things they wear in Paris. And you don't look well in those clothes, Isabelle. You know you don't. Even I don't look well in them. How could one? Hand me the scissors, would you. (ISABELLE *looks around.*) There. Right behind you. (*Impatient.*) On the table. (ISABELLE *stands up and drops everything.*) What's the matter with you? (*She rings the small round bell. Pulling* ISABELLE *up, as she bends to pick up the seed pearls.*) Really, Isabelle. (LEA *comes in from the kitchen.* MADAME DANZARD *points to the floor.* LEA *kneels and starts collecting the tiny seed pearls that have fallen.* MADAME DANZARD *eyes the floor, making sure every last seed pearl has been picked up.*) Besides, I don't like to leave the house.

ISABELLE. But why, Maman? What could happen to it?

MADAME DANZARD. A lot can happen to a house

when you're not there. And then—going to Paris—such a trip.

ISABELLE. A trip!

MADAME DANZARD. And such an expense. Think of the money. Mmm—Paris.

ISABELLE. Paris!

MADAME DANZARD. Yes, I think we'll just have to skip Paris this year. (*A bell rings.* MADAME DANZARD *and* ISABELLE *jump.* LEA *goes to the door.*)

ISABELLE. Who's that?

MADAME DANZARD. Shhh. Let *me* listen. Who could it be? In this weather. (ISABELLE *puts her evening bag back into the sewing basket. She and* MADAME DANZARD *hurriedly sit down on the couch and wait, smiling, rubbing their cheeks to redden them.* LEA *comes back with the mail. She puts one letter in her pocket quickly, enters the sitting room with another letter on a tray. She presents the tray to* MADAME DANZARD *with a letter opener.*) Oh! Mail. (*She takes the letter.* LEA *goes up the stairs.*)

ISABELLE. Anything for me, Maman?

MADAME DANZARD. Look at this. Would you look at this, Isabelle. No return address. And look at that hand-writing. What do you think it could be? (*She waves the letter toward* ISABELLE.)

ISABELLE. (*Taking the letter.*) Well, it's not a marriage.

MADAME DANZARD. (*Snatching it back. Excitedly.*) Maybe a funeral. Whose I wonder?

ISABELLE. What is it, Maman? (LEA *comes into the up-stairs room, sits down on the bed, opens the letter and eagerly begins reading it.*)

MADAME DANZARD. (*Eagerly opening the letter.*) Just a minute. Just a minute. (*Crushed.*) Another letter from the Little Shepherds of Le Mans. Will they never stop asking for money. Those children must be eating out of golden bowls. (*Reflecting suddenly.*) Hmm. I wonder how much the Blanchards are giving.

ISABELLE. (*Staring out at the rain.*) Do you really think it will rain straight through the winter?

MADAME DANZARD. You can never tell. But it looks it, doesn't it? (*Going to stand beside* ISABELLE.) It certainly looks it. Rain, rain, rain. Those clouds. I've never seen it so grey. Well, don't complain, Isabelle. At least we don't have to go out. (*She walks out of the room.* ISABELLE *follows her.* CHRISTINE *finishes putting everything away in the kitchen and goes upstairs into their room.* LEA, *hastily folding up the letter, looks at her guiltily.*)

CHRISTINE. (*Softly.*) What is it, Lea? Another letter from Maman? (LEA *looks away. Gently.*) Well, go on. Read it. There's no reason to stop just because I came into the room. (*She takes off her long apron and folds it neatly.*)

LEA. I'll read it later.

CHRISTINE. You won't have time later. You're exhausted by ten. Read it now. (LEA *looks at her. Smiling.*) Why don't you read it out loud?

LEA. (*Nervously.*) Do you really want me to?

CHRISTINE. I wouldn't say it otherwise, would I?

LEA. (*Unfolding the letter, begins to read.*) "Lea, my pet, my little dove. I know I'll see you Sunday as usual, but I miss you. Little Lea. You'll always be little."

CHRISTINE. Go on.

LEA. (*Continuing.*) "Don't forget to bring me the money. You forgot last week."

CHRISTINE. Poor Maman.

LEA. Christine—Maman just—

CHRISTINE. Maman just what? (*Changing. Gentle.*) Go ahead. Keep reading.

LEA. (*Going on with the letter.*) "You can't wear your hair that way anymore, Lea. Like a child. All that long hair." (*She stops.*)

CHRISTINE. Well? Don't leave anything out.

LEA. (*Going on.*) "Next Sunday, when you come, I'll fix it for you. It'll be better that way. Like Christine's. Won't fall in the soup." (LEA *looks up, laughing.* CHRISTINE *doesn't smile.*) (*Going back to the letter. Quickly.*) "Or get Christine to fix it for you. But--" (*She stops.*)

CHRISTINE. But what?

LEA. "Tell her to be gentle."

CHRISTINE. (*Snatching the letter from* LEA.) I'm never going back.

LEA. Christine.

CHRISTINE. (*Folding the letter up very small.*) You can go if you want to.

LEA. You know I wouldn't without you.

CHRISTINE. But you still care for her. She loves you.

LEA. But Christine, Christine. Maman loves you too. She's just . . .

CHRISTINE. What?

LEA. . . . scared of you.

CHRISTINE. Scared of me? (*Giving the tiny folded up letter back to* LEA.) You never stick up for me. But that's right. Defend her. Take her part. Like you always do. (*Moving away.*) Once she said that just to look at me made her sick. She couldn't even keep me after the first year. She hated when I cried.

LEA. Christine.

CHRISTINE. At Saint Mary of the Fields, I used to escape. Once a month. No one in this town would have brought me back—you know what they call it here. But your Maman— our Maman— she brought me back every time. In the end all I wanted was to be a nun. A nun! (*She smiles.*) That's all I wanted. But then of course she took me out. She hadn't expected that. That was against all her plans. I had to work. I had to make money. And she kept all of it. She placed me — and each time I got used to it, she took me out again. Sometimes I'd run away. I ran back to the Sisters. They wanted to keep me. It was Maman, our beloved precious Maman, who would come and drag me out again.

LEA. Don't be angry with me.

CHRISTINE. I'm not angry with you.

LEA. Your face. It looks so —

CHRISTINE. (*Cutting in.*) What? What's the matter with my face?

LEA. It just looked . . . Your face is beautiful. There's nothing wrong with your face.

CHRISTINE. No? (*She takes the hairbrush.*) I'll fix it for you. Just like she said. I'll fix it. (*Tenderly starting to brush* LEA'S *hair. Longingly.*) If we didn't go back we could have all our Sundays together, just to ourselves. We could walk, we could go to the station and watch the trains come in. We could sit in the square, we could — But no — you wouldn't want that, would you? You want to go back. Don't you? (*Pleading.*) Don't you, Lea? (LEA *is silent.* CHRISTINE *changes, violently brushes* LEA'S *hair.*) Of course you do. (*Roughly, she twists* LEA'S *hair into two buns on either side of her face.*) There. Like this. That's what she meant. (*Pulling* LEA *over to the mirror above the sink. Raging.*) Look. How do you like it?

LEA. (*Tearing out her hair and sobbing.*) I hate it. (*She grabs the brush from* CHRISTINE *and tries to fix her own hair, putting it back the way it was. She does this clumsily, jerkily — too upset to get it right.* CHRISTINE *watches her in silence, suddenly overwhelmed at what she has done.*)

CHRISTINE. I am a monster — aren't I? Just like she says.

LEA. You're not a monster. (*She stops fixing her hair.*)

CHRISTINE. Here. Let me. (*Cautiously, she reaches for the brush.* LEA *hesitates, turns away.*) I'll do it for you. (LEA *still hesitates.*) Let me do it—please. (LEA *is silent.*) Please. (*Tentatively,* LEA *holds out the brush.* CHRISTINE *takes it from her gently. Softly, slowly, she starts brushing* LEA'S *hair.*) What did you mean when you said my face was beautiful?

LEA. What I said.

CHRISTINE. What's beautiful about it? Tell me one thing.

LEA. (*Looking up at her.*) Your eyes.

SCENE 4

The sound of a radio. In the sitting room MADAME DANZARD *is turning the dial of a radio. She stops at a station which is playing the overture of Offenbach's "La Vie Parisienne." She smiles. She stands beside the radio, listening, and starts humming along. She goes over to the dining room cabinet and takes out an old photograph album. She looks through the album, sighing to herself, gently tapping her foot. She puts the album down on the table in front of the couch and begins dancing to the music.* ISABELLE *comes down the stairs, slowly at first, then quicker, interrupting* MADAME DANZARD'S *dance. Startled,* MADAME DANZARD *immediately switches to a station playing a Bach organ prelude.* She looks at Isabelle.* ISABELLE *walks across the room and takes a chocolate out of a glass bowl, puts it into her mouth and looks at her mother.* MADAME DANZARD *snatches the bowl away and puts it in the dining*

*Nun Komm der Heiden Heiland (BWV659) a 2 Clav. e Pedale J.S. Bach.

room cabinet. ISABELLE *sits down on the couch and starts looking through the photograph album.* MADAME DANZARD *takes a white glove from the cabinet and carefully puts it on. She rings the small round bell.* LEA *hurries in. She stands silently as* MADAME DANZARD, *wearing her white glove, slowly goes all around the room, testing the furniture and mouldings for dust.* LEA *smiles as* MADAME DANZARD *checks. On the radio, the Bach prelude continues.* MADAME DANZARD *walks up the staircase, smiling, checking the banister, kneeling down and touching the balustrades.* CHRISTINE *comes into the kitchen, carrying a heavy pewter pitcher with dried flowers.* MADAME DANZARD, *bending down in an awkward position on the staircase, finds a spot of dust on the white glove, stands up, shows it to* LEA. MADAME DANZARD *removes the glove, puts it on the table on the landing and goes downstairs to the dining room.* LEA *rushes up the stairs to clean the place where the dust has been found.* CHRISTINE *comes into the dining room, carrying the pitcher of dried flowers.* MADAME DANZARD *checks the flowers, rearranges one or two.* CHRISTINE *takes the pewter pitcher upstairs to their table on the landing. She picks up the white glove, looks at* LEA *dusting the staircase. Their hands touch for an instant.* CHRISTINE *goes down the stairs and out the hallway carrying the white glove, as* LEA *continues up the stairs dusting between the railings of the banister.* MADAME DANZARD *goes over to the radio and turns it off.*

ISABELLE. Who's this, Maman?
MADAME DANZARD. (*Looking over* ISABELLE'S *shoulder.*) Ah. You great aunt Dominique, whom you never knew. Lucky for you. (*Sitting down beside* ISABELLE *on the couch.*) She owned half the houses on the Rue Dutois. When your father and I were first mar-

ried, she wouldn't take one franc off the rent. That's the mentality of the people on your father's side. (*Pointing.*) That dress! Always pretending to be poor as church mice. (*Turning the page.*) Ah. The Rue Dutois. A quiet street. Almost as quiet as this one.

ISABELLE. No street is as quiet as this one.

MADAME DANZARD. (*Turning the page.*) Oh. Look at you. Right here in the courtyard. Do you still have that little hat? Why don't you ever wear that little hat anymore, Isabelle?

ISABELLE. What hat? Oh. That hat. Of course not, Maman.

MADAME DANZARD. Too bad. You were delightful in that hat.

ISABELLE. Maman, do you know how old I was then?

MADAME DANZARD. (*Looking closely at the photograph.*) Oh yes. Yes. I suppose so, Isabelle. I suppose you were.

ISABELLE. Exactly. (MADAME DANZARD *turns the page.*)

MADAME DANZARD. Here you are again. Here *we* are. Oh look! (*Together they laugh over the photographs.* MADAME DANZARD, *still chuckling, continues to turn the pages of the photograph album. Suddenly* ISABELLE *smiles. She stifles a laugh.* MADAME DANZARD *looks up.* ISABELLE *begins laughing in earnest.* MADAME DANZARD *sees the photograph* ISABELLE *is looking at and stops laughing immediately. She slams the photograph album shut.* ISABELLE, *trying to stifle her laughter, leaves the room. After a few moments* MADAME DANZARD *goes up the stairs on tiptoe, silently opens the door to* CHRISTINE *and* LEA'S *room, one foot stepping in, and stares at the immaculate perfect order, as the light dims.*

SCENE 5

LEA *and* CHRISTINE *come into their room, wearing their faded dresses and coats of the first scene.*

CHRISTINE. I don't want to force you.

LEA. You're not forcing me. We can never go back.

CHRISTINE. She didn't mean you when she told us to get out. She only meant me. (*She takes off her coat.*)

LEA. She meant both of us.

CHRISTINE. Not you, Lea. Not ever you. She'll never stop loving you.

LEA. She'll never forgive me for the money. Never, Christine. You know she won't.

CHRISTINE. But why shouldn't you keep your own money—instead of giving it to her. (LEA *sits on the bed, upset.*) She'll forgive you. You'll see. She'll forgive you. She always has. (*Looking at* LEA.) And Lea, Lea, you know what we'll do with that money? (LEA *is silent.*) We'll save it. We'll save all of it from now on. We'll put it together— yours and mine—and save it. And someday, Lea, someday we'll—we'll—(LEA *looks at her.*)

LEA. Remember what you said—we could spend all our Sundays together.

CHRISTINE. I remember.

LEA. Promise?

CHRISTINE. Promise. (LEA *picks up the small blanket from their mother. She bites the wool with her teeth, loosening a strand. She pulls it, stops, pulls it again.*)

LEA. Here. Hold this. (*She hands* CHRISTINE *the blanket.*)

CHRISTINE. What are you doing? (LEA *keeps pulling.*)
You've had that since you were four. (*As* LEA *pulls, the
loosely crocheted blanket begins to unravel.*) Lea!

LEA. Just hold it. (*She pulls harder.*) Now pull from
your end. (CHRISTINE *hesitates.*) Go ahead. Pull it!

CHRISTINE. But—

LEA. Go on. (CHRISTINE *cautiously begins to pull.*)
That's it! That's right. Go ahead. Pull it. Pull it. Pull it
harder. (CHRISTINE *looks at her.*) Harder. (CHRISTINE
really starts pulling in earnest.) That's it. Harder.
Oh harder. (*She pulls from her end.*) Harder. (*As the
blanket unravels faster and faster, they run around the
room. They are constricted by the confines of the narrow
room. They wind the wool around the bed, the
sink. They wind it around each other.* LEA, *laughing,
falls on the bed.* CHRISTINE *falls beside her.*)

CHRISTINE. (*Laughing.*) No more, no more. (LEA
wraps CHRISTINE *even closer to her with the wool.*)
(Breaking away suddenly.) That's enough. I have to go
downstairs.

LEA. It's not time yet. (*Playful.*) Don't you want to
play anymore?

CHRISTINE. (*Putting on her apron. Abruptly.*) No.

SCENE 6

MADAME DANZARD *comes down the hall, dressed to go
out. She is holding two hats. In the maid's room,*
CHRISTINE *is sitting on the bed, embroidering a
white chemise with delicate lace and wide intricate
shoulder straps.* LEA *sits beside her, hemming a
long white nightgown.*

MADAME DANZARD. (*Calling.*) Isabelle! Isabelle. (ISABELLE *comes into the dining room.* MADAME DANZARD *holds out a particularly provincial hat.*) Charming, isn't it? (ISABELLE *is silent.*) Well, go ahead. There's no reason to be shy. (*She lunges toward* ISABELLE *with the hat.*)

ISABELLE. (*Drawing back.*) Oh. It's for me, Maman?

MADAME DANZARD. Of course it's for you. For whom else?

ISABELLE. And you want me to wear it now?

MADAME DANZARD. (*Very serious.*) I don't want you to wear anything else. You haven't forgotten how pretentious the Loupins looked last Sunday in their monstrosities.

ISABELLE. I remember.

MADAME DANZARD. Well, I can't wait to see their faces today. (ISABELLE *puts on the hat.*) Perfect. (*The bell rings.*)

ISABELLE. (*Anxious.*) It's them!

MADAME DANZARD. Early, as usual. Hoping to catch a glimpse of something. Well, they won't see anything today. They'll just have to wait. (*She stands still for a few moments, delightedly looking at her watch. She puts on another hat, if anything even more provincial than* ISABELLE'S. *Plunging in the stickpin of the hat.*) How do you like mine?

ISABELLE. (*After a pause.*) Adorable.

MADAME DANZARD. Well together—I must say—we make quite a pair. (*The bell rings again. They go out.*)

LEA. I'll never sew like you. Look at this hem. (*She holds up the nightgown and laughs.*) Even my hems are crooked. All those years with the Sisters and I never learned.

CHRISTINE. The Sisters didn't know how to teach you.

Give it to me. I'll do it. (LEA *gives her the nightgown.*) Remember when I used to visit you at the convent? You waited for me at the gate. You were so little and so hungry all the time. (*She laughs.*) You're still hungry all the time.

LEA. Christine.

CHRISTINE. Hmm?

LEA. Can I . . .

CHRISTINE. (*Knowing what* LEA *wants.*) Can you what?

LEA. Can I look at them again?

CHRISTINE. Of course you can. They're yours. (LEA *jumps up and pulls an old trunk out from under the bed.* CHRISTINE *smiles.* LEA *pulls up the lid. The trunk is overflowing with beautiful white lingerie, undergarments trimmed with lace, nightgowns with fluttering ribbons, delicate ruffled chemises.*)

LEA. (*Gathering it all in her arms.*) All of it! All of it! No one sews like you. (CHRISTINE *stops sewing, watches* LEA.) Oh Christine. I can't believe how beautiful they are. (*She buries her face in the clothing.*)

CHRISTINE. (*Holding up the chemise she was sewing.*) Look, it's almost finished.

LEA. (*Raising her head.*) Already?

CHRISTINE. Yes. Come try it on.

LEA. Now?

CHRISTINE. Don't you want to?

LEA. I want to.

CHRISTINE. Well then. (LEA *comes forward.*) Go ahead. I'll close my eyes. (*She looks at* LEA.) I want to be surprised. (*She closes her eyes.* LEA *takes off her dress and slowly, carefully, puts on the chemise.*)

LEA. Christine . . . you can look now.

CHRISTINE. Can I?
LEA. Yes. (CHRISTINE *opens her eyes.*) It's beautiful.
CHRISTINE. It's you who are beautiful.
LEA. (*Tentatively reaching out her hand.*) I'm cold.
CHRISTINE. (*Going toward her.*) I know.

SCENE 7

Light comes up on the empty sitting room. Offstage
ISABELLE *is playing "Sur Le Pont D'Avignon" badly*
on the piano. She hums off key to the music, con-
tinuing to make mistakes as she goes along. Abrupt-
ly, the music stops. ISABELLE *peeks her head out in-*
to the sitting room. She comes in and goes over to
the dining room cabinet. She opens the cabinet and
takes out the glass bowl of chocolates. She takes
one, unwraps it and gobbles it up. She takes
another, unwraps it, pops it into her mouth. LEA
comes in, carrying a dusting cloth. She sees
ISABELLE *with the chocolate in her mouth.* ISABELLE
looks away, awkwardly chewing the chocolate. LEA
begins dusting the couch. ISABELLE *takes a chocolate*
from the bowl and, hesitatingly, holds it out to LEA.
LEA *doesn't move.* ISABELLE *continues to hold out the*
chocolate. LEA *hesitates, cautiously looks around. She*
looks back at the chocolate, still hesitating. Suddenly
she snatches the chocolate and puts the glass bowl back
in the cabinet and leaves. LEA *goes up the staircase to*
the landing. She takes the chocolate out of her pocket,
smiles to herself. CHRISTINE *comes into the kitchen,*
holding a mortar and pestle. She starts pounding. Off-
stage ISABELLE *begins playing "Sur Le Pont*
D'Avignon"

with one finger on the piano. She plays quickly, badly.
LEA *begins dusting the banister. Accidentally she hits
the pewter pitcher. It rolls off the table and clatters
down the stairs. The dried flowers scatter.*

LEA. (*Closing her eyes and screaming.*) CHRISTINE!
(*In the kitchen* CHRISTINE *stops pounding instantly. She
runs to the stairs.*)

CHRISTINE. What's wrong? What happened?

LEA. (*Frantic.*) The pitcher. The pewter pitcher.
Madame will be so angry. Madame will—

CHRISTINE. Shhh. (*She goes down on her knees and
apprehensively, picks up the pitcher.*) Look, Lea. Come
here. It's not even broken. (LEA, *unbelievingly, opens her
eyes, goes down the stairs to* CHRISTINE.) My angel, my
dove. (*She pulls* LEA *down beside her.*) Don't be frightened.
Look at me. Look. (*The bell rings. The piano stops.* LEA
looks into CHRISTINE'S *eyes.* CHRISTINE *gathers the dried
flowers and puts them back in the pewter pitcher.*) Don't
worry. Nothing is broken. Believe me. (ISABELLE *appears
and sees* LEA *and* CHRISTINE. LEA *rushes down the hall.*
CHRISTINE *puts the pewter pitcher back on the table on the
landing. She comes down the stairs, goes to open the front
door.* ISABELLE *goes after her.* MADAME DANZARD *comes
into the house.* ISABELLE *runs ahead.* CHRISTINE *goes out
the hall.*)

ISABELLE. Anything for me, Maman? (MADAME DAN-
ZARD *takes off her hat. She smiles delightedly, raises her
finger in anticipation. She puts her hat, gloves, coat,
bag and package on the dining room table. Smiling with
excitement she opens the package.* ISABELLE *leans forward expectantly. Happily,* MADAME DANZARD *holds up
a photograph in a frame. It is a picture of herself and*
ISABELLE *in their two hats.* ISABELLE *looks at the
photograph and grimaces.* MADAME DANZARD *sets the
photograph down on the radio table. She turns on the*

radio, as ISABELLE *takes the clothing and wrapping paper off the dining room table.* "C'est La Saison D'Amour"* *blares out over the radio.* MADAME DANZARD *smiles, bursts into song. Blackout.*)

SCENE 8

LEA *and* CHRISTINE *stand side by side. They are dressed identically in dark wool dresses. Each dress has a wide yolk of intricate white lace. Their hair is arranged in exactly the same way. Their eyes are wide. They look frightened, shy. They have come to have their photograph taken.*

LEA. (*Whispering.*) Do you really think we should have come?

CHRISTINE. Why not? I wanted a photograph of you—of us together.

LEA. Suppose someone should find out?

CHRISTINE. Suppose they should? We're allowed to have a photograph taken, aren't we?

LEA. It's so expensive.

CHRISTINE. We can afford it.

LEA. I'm nervous.

CHRISTINE. (*Holding her hand for a moment.*) It's all right.

LEA. My hair—is it—

CHRISTINE. It's perfect.

LEA. But did you get it right on top?

*"C'est La Saison D'Amour" Copyright © 1936 by Musikverlag und Bühnenvertrieb Zürich, A.G. Zurich. Reproduit avec l'autorisation de "ROYALTY" Editions Musicales, 25, Rue d'Hauteville, Paris. Musique de Oscar Straus d'après Johann Strauss père. Paroles de Albert Willemetz et Léopold Marchand.

CHRISTINE. You look like an angel. I'm going to fix it like that every Sunday.

LEA. I hate that iron.

CHRISTINE. Shhh. He's coming back.

LEA. Oh Christine, I'm frightened.

CHRISTINE. Of what? It's only a photograph. (*For a moment she clasps her hands tightly together. She straightens her dress.*) We should have done it long ago.

PHOTOGRAPHER. (*Voice over.*) I'm sorry that took so long. Now look this way. That's right. You're sisters, aren't you?

CHRISTINE. Yes.

PHOTOGRAPHER. (*Voice over.*) I knew right away. This should make a lovely photograph. Just step a little closer to each other. (CHRISTINE *and* LEA *move very close.*) Not quite so close. (*They move slightly apart.*) That's it. Perfect. Don't move. (*There is a burst of light as he takes the photograph.*) Did your mother always dress you like that? (*They are silent.*) Hmmm?

CHRISTINE. Like what?

PHOTOGRAPHER. (*Voice over.*) In the same clothes.

CHRISTINE. She never did.

PHOTOGRAPHER. (*Voice over.*) You look like twins. (LEA *smiles.*) No, not twins. But sisters. Sisters, certainly. Such a resemblance.

CHRISTINE. We're not twins. I'm six years older than my sister.

PHOTOGRAPHER. (*Voice over.*) Six years? Look up please. (*Again there is a burst of light.*) You look practically the same. But I guess a lot of people have told you that.

CHRISTINE. Some.

PHOTOGRAPHER. (*Voice over.*) Not very talkative, are you? What about your sister? Cat got her tongue?

CHRISTINE. (*Warningly.*) She's shy.

PHOTOGRAPHER. (*Voice over.*) Well, I've always wanted a sister — shy or not. (LEA *looks in the direction of the* PHOTOGRAPHER.) A sister sticks by you. Even when you're in trouble. Isn't that true? (LEA *smiles.*) Can she talk? Such a shy thing. I bet you're your mother's favorite.

LEA. (*Nervously.*) No . . . I . . .

PHOTOGRAPHER. (*Voice over.*) Still a child, isn't she? I can see that. What a sweet smile. Please now, both of you smile. And look at me. (LEA *smiles.* CHRISTINE *looks directly at the* PHOTOGRAPHER.) That's good. (*There is a burst of light, as he takes the final photograph.*) That will be fine. No one would ever know the two of you were servants. At the Danzards, aren't you?

CHRISTINE. (*Nervous.*) Yes.

PHOTOGRAPHER. (*Voice over.*) Excellent people, the Danzards. I've known them for years. Photographed the whole family. Photographed the daughter when she was just a child. (*He pauses.*) I hear she's going to be married soon. (CHRISTINE *and* LEA *are silent.*) Of course I've been hearing that for years. (*He waits. They don't speak.*) Well — seeing is believing I always say. Who knows if it's true. (*They remain silent. He chuckles quietly.*) You two certainly are discreet. They're lucky to have two such discreet young ladies. Especially in this town.

CHRISTINE. Hurry, Lea. I still have the shopping to do. (*She puts on her coat.*)

PHOTOGRAPHER. (*Voice over.*) You've been there a long time, haven't you? (*They are silent.*) How many years is it now?

CHRISTINE. A few.

PHOTOGRAPHER. (*Voice over.*) I'm sure they treat you well. (*They remain silent.*) Very fine people. Excellent people. But of course you know that.

CHRISTINE. Certainly, we know it. Come Lea, don't be so slow. (LEA *turns her back to the* PHOTOGRAPHER *and puts on her coat. It is exactly the same as* CHRISTINE'S.)

PHOTOGRAPHER. (*Voice over.*) No need to be shy with me. (*He laughs.*) Madame Danzard makes you work hard enough, I imagine. For the money she pays you. (CHRISTINE, *eagar to leave, starts taking out her money.*)

CHRISTINE. You said fifty francs, didn't you?

PHOTOGRAPHER. (*Voice over.*) For you girls, I'll make it twenty-five. You can pay me when you come for the photograph.

CHRISTINE. Fifty is what you said, fifty is what we pay.

PHOTOGRAPHER. (*Voice over.*) I see. Very well. Come back in two weeks.

LEA. (*Smiling.*) Thank you. (*They go out.*)

SCENE 9

Before the scene opens, the slap of cards hitting a table is heard. Light comes up on MADAME DAN-ZARD *and* ISABELLE *sitting at the dining room table. They are each armed with a pack of fifty-two cards. They sit facing each other. They are engaged in playing an elaborate game of réussite, a card game similar to double solitaire, the difference being that with réussite, each player secretly asks a question about the future before the game starts. Whether the question is answered affirmatively or not depends on the outcome of the game. When the scene opens,* MADAME DANZARD *and* ISABELLE *are laying out the last row of cards. As all but three cards are used from the very beginning, the cards almost completely cover the table.*)

MADAME DANZARD. (*As she finishes laying out her cards, deftly, neatly, straightening them as she goes along.*) What did you wish for this time? If you don't tell, you won't get it.

ISABELLE. (*Sloppier as she finishes laying out her cards.*) That's not true. You don't have to tell what you wish for.

MADAME DANZARD. Well, I think I can guess. I'm not telling my wish either. Not even if I win.

ISABELLE. Ready Maman?

MADAME DANZARD. I'm ready. But you're not. Look at those cards.

ISABELLE. which cards?

MADAME DANZARD. Those over there. They're going to fall off the table. (ISABELLE *straightens the last cards.*) Good. Now we're ready. (*She and* ISABELLE *tap their remaining cards on the table three times.*)

ISABELLE. One, two, three . . . begin. Maman—that is not fair.

MADAME DANZARD. What's not fair?

ISABELLE. You started at two.

MADAME DANZARD. I did not. I absolutely did not. However, if you insist, we'll start again.

ISABELLE. One . . . two . . . three . . . start.

MADAME DANZARD. (*Inspecting her cards.*) I don't have anything to start with.

ISABELLE. You always do that. Start first.

MADAME DANZARD. Never. That's your imagination.

ISABELLE. (*Shrieking.*) I saw you.

MADAME DANZARD. Quiet, Isabelle. (*Looking at her cards.*) This is absurd. I can't move a thing. (*She looks over at* ISABELLE's *cards.* ISABELLE *sits pondering.*) Look at you. You have a million things. Don't you see? (*Disgusted.*) Aah.

ISABELLE. Where Maman?

MADAME DANZARD. There. Right there. Right before your eyes. Oh, Isabelle, sometimes you're so slow.

ISABELLE. You think so, Maman?

MADAME DANZARD. Well I'm stuck. Wait a minute. Why didn't I see that seven. Just a minute now. (*She transfers a large block of cards.*) That certainly should make things a little easier. (*Looking at* ISABELLE'S *cards.*) What's happening over there? That six is still sitting there.

ISABELLE. I see it, Maman. (*She moves the six.*)

MADAME DANZARD. (*Directing as* ISABELLE *moves her cards.*) And now the nine. Go ahead.

ISABELLE. What nine?

MADAME DANZARD. The nine of diamonds onto the ten of clubs. What's the matter with you?

ISABELLE. Maman please. I can't concentrate.

MADAME DANZARD. What are you talking about? Of course you can concentrate. This is a game of concentration. You have to concentrate. You have to concentrate on every little detail. Otherwise all will be lost. (*Looking over her own cards like a hawk. Excited.*) Red eight on black nine on red ten on—Perfect! That frees my queen and now I can take all these with the jack—(*She lifts a huge block of cards.*)—put them on the queen and . . . let's see what's under here. What's been hiding from me. (*She turns up a card. Disappointed.*) Three of spades. Now what am I going to do with that? (*Suddenly.*) You got an ace, Isabelle. How did that happen? Clubs. My two is buried under that nine. I'll never get it out.

ISABELLE. I've got it, Maman. Look. And the three.

MADAME DANZARD. How did you get them so fast? (ISABELLE *laughs gleefully.*) You're not cheating, are you?

ISABELLE. Maman.

MADAME DANZARD. (*Checking the cards.*) Where is the ace of diamonds? Where is that ace?

ISABELLE. Not the ace of diamonds, Maman. But I've got the ace of spades. And the two, and the—

MADAME DANZARD. Three!

ISABELLE. (*Overlapping and getting there first.*) Three!

MADAME DANZARD. Isabelle! How could you. Blocked again. Incredible.

ISABELLE. What are we having for dinner tonight, Maman?

MADAME DANZARD. Blanquette of veal.

ISABELLE. Veal again?

MADAME DANZARD. (*Looking at her watch.*) They'll be down soon. Ah—there's the four. (*Slapping down the four of spades.*) They never speak anymore. Have you noticed? Not a word. The older one walks by me as if I'm not there. (LEA *comes into the upstairs room, lays a delicate, handmade white coverlet on their bed, places the photograph of herself and* CHRISTINE *taken at the PHOTOGRAPHER'S on the night table, and goes out again.*)

ISABELLE. I have the five. And the six! The older one was always that way.

MADAME DANZARD. (*Slapping down her cards.*) Seven, eight!

ISABELLE. (*Tapping her mother on the hand.*) One hand, Maman!

MADAME DANZARD. Every Sunday—up in that room alone—it's amazing.

ISABELLE. They've always stuck to themselves.

MADAME DANZARD. They haven't seen their mother in years.

ISABELLE. (*Looking at her mother. Quietly.*) That's just as well.

MADAME DANZARD. You know—I found the older one in the hallway trying to rub a stain off the door.

ISABELLE. I know that stain. It's been there for years. It'll never come off.

MADAME DANZARD. And she knows it. (*Smacking down three more cards as* ISABELLE *shrieks.*) And the nine, ten, jack! (*She takes a small tidbit from a dish on the table and pops it into her mouth. Making a face.*) What's wrong with her? She's put too much salt in these again.

ISABELLE. (*Laying down a card.*) The queen!

MADAME DANZARD. Have you turned up your three cards yet?

ISABELLE. Not yet. (*She sneaks a card into her lap.*)

MADAME DANZARD. Well, I absolutely refuse to turn—Isabelle! You cheated. I can't believe my eyes.

ISABELLE. I did not.

MADAME DANZARD. You did. You moved that jack of hearts onto the queen of diamonds.

ISABELLE. And—?

MADAME DANZARD. What do you mean—And? You know you can't move red onto red. Move it back.

ISABELLE. It was there before, Maman. I started the whole game that way.

MADAME DANZARD. Isabelle, please stop this lying at once. And just what was happening at the Blanchards the other night?

ISABELLE. Nothing was happening, Maman.

MADAME DANZARD. Nothing? Of course they're so blind—(ISABELLE *sneaks her ace of hearts onto the edge of the table.*) But with a marriage coming, you can't just smile at anyone.

ISABELLE. I wasn't smiling, Maman.

MADAME DANZARD. No? Wait! You put out the ace of hearts without even telling me. Where's my two?

Here it is. My two, my three. (*She slaps them down.*) Where's that four?

ISABELLE. Here Maman. I have it. (*She puts it down.*)

MADAME DANZARD. You don't? You do. Well, I'm turning over my three cards. It's finally come to that. (*She turns up one of the three cards.*) Jacks of hearts. What use is he? Looks just like Jacques Blanchard, doesn't he? Not a place for him here. (*Looking at her watch again.*) Where are they? Have they forgotten the Flintons are coming? What's wrong with them? Do you know that yesterday, coming back from the Loupins, I saw them sitting in the square. At eleven o'clock in the morning! Can you believe that?

ISABELLE. Unbelievable.

MADAME DANZARD. Eleven o'clock in the morning. I didn't say anything when they came back. But they knew. (*She turns over the second card.*) Four of diamonds. Too soon for that. Should I look at the third one? Yes or no?

ISABELLE. Go ahead Maman. Take a chance. (MADAME *turns over her last card. It is the ace of hearts. She smacks it down in the center.*)

MADAME DANZARD. (*Ecstatic.*) Hearts! Just what I was waiting for.

ISABELLE. (*Slapping down an ace of diamonds.*) Diamonds!

MADAME DANZARD. What?

ISABELLE. My ace, my two, my—

MADAME DANZARD. I can't do a thing till you move that queen.

ISABELLE. Queen? What queen?

MADAME DANZARD. Your queen, your queen. Use your eyes, Isabelle. (*She stands up and moves* ISABELLE'S *queen into the center.*)

ISABELLE. (*Watching her mother.*) There. My queen.

MADAME DANZARD. And *my* king! That frees everything. Now we can really go ahead! (*The game builds to a frenzied finish with* ISABELLE *feverishly maneuvering her cards, and* MADAME DANZARD *laughing wildly and madly slapping down card after card with amazing speed. Reaching the end of the game, she triumphantly hugs the despairing* ISABELLE. LEA *comes down the stairs wearing a pale pink sweater. She places a lace cloth on the table in front of the couch.*)

ISABELLE. (*Whispering to her mother.*) Maman, do you see? (LEA *looks up, aware they are whispering about her.*)

MADAME DANZARD. Of course I see. What do you think I am — blind? What in heaven's name allows her to think she can wear a sweater like that in this house. (LEA *clumsily finishes laying down the lace cloth and goes to the kitchen. In the kitchen,* CHRISTINE *is preparing dough for a tart. She stops when she sees* LEA.)

LEA. You told me I could wear it.

CHRISTINE. When I gave it to you, I never told you to wear it in this house, did I? I never told you to wear it downstairs. (LEA *is silent.* CHRISTINE *goes back to kneading the dough.*)

MADAME DANZARD. Just where did she think she was going? And how did she have the nerve, the extreme nerve to buy such a thing?

ISABELLE. Maman —

CHRISTINE. (*Wetting the dough too much, her hands getting messy.*) Why did you? Why would you want to wear that sweater anywhere but in our room? What were you thinking?

MADAME DANZARD. What is the world coming to? I couldn't believe my eyes.

ISABELLE. But Maman —

LEA. I wasn't thinking of anything but us. (*Carefully,*

she takes off the sweater.)

CHRISTINE. (*Pulling her violently into a corner of the kitchen.*) You're lying.

MADAME DANZARD. There are no buts involved here.

CHRISTINE. Don't think I haven't noticed. I have eyes. I can see. When I come into the dining room, you're polishing the table looking off into nowhere. When you sew, you prick your fingers, when you wax the floor, you get the wax on your shoes. You drop plates, you spill water, you chip cups, you burn yourself with the iron—

LEA. I dropped that plate six weeks ago.

CHRISTINE. What about the cup?

LEA. The cup was chipped when we came here. I do things. I get things done.

CHRISTINE. (*Wiping her dough covered hands on her apron.*) But you look good. That I can see. Your apron neat as a pin. Immaculate. (*She circles* LEA.) The collar just right in front. The cuffs folded just so. You keep yourself perfect, don't you? And why?

LEA. I've always dressed this way. Look at me. We've always dressed this way.

CHRISTINE. You're different. Believe me. I know. (CHRISTINE *goes out the hall.* LEA *follows her.*)

ISABELLE. Maybe she didn't know, Maman.

MADAME DANZARD. (*Gathering up the cards.*) Of course she knew. She deliberately put it on and wore it. That sweater must have cost—

ISABELLE. (*Interrupting.*) Maybe—

MADAME DANZARD. I wonder if I pay them too much.

ISABELLE. Maybe she didn't buy it, Maman.

MADAME DANZARD. What?

ISABELLE. (*Rising and walking to the staircase.*) Maybe it wasn't her.

MADAME DANZARD. What are you talking about?
Make yourself clear, Isabelle.

ISABELLE. Maybe it was her sister who gave her that
sweater. Didn't you see? It was handmade.

MADAME DANZARD. (*Softly.*) Oh. Yes. Yes. Now I see.
(*Softer yet.*) I believe you're right, Isabelle.

ISABELLE. I think so, Maman.

MADAME DANZARD. Handmade! Of course. And
such expensive wool. I saw wool just like that in the
Dupin's shop window. You don't think she bought it there,
do you?

ISABELLE. Maybe, Maman. I wouldn't be surprised.

MADAME DANZARD. What an extravagance! Can you
imagine if someone had seen . . .

ISABELLE. (*Standing up.*) Oh Maman, you go too far.
(*She starts up the staircase.*)

MADAME DANZARD. (*Following her.*) Do I? Do I, my
dear? You don't know this town like I do. Imagine if the
Flintons had been here? Or Madame Blanchard. Or . . .
I can't even think of it . . . Madame Castelneuve. You
think I go too far. No my dear, you haven't lived here
nearly long enough.

SCENE 10

It is night. Silence. LEA *moans in the darkness.*

CHRISTINE. Lea.

LEA. I can't breathe.

CHRISTINE. Lea.

LEA. I can't breathe. I can't. (*Light comes up in their
room.*) Someone behind me, pulling my coat. Even before I
turn around I know. She grabs my hand and starts running.
Her hand like iron around mine. I make myself heavy, but
she holds me tight and I can feel all her little bones. She

snatches me into the house and I run from corner to corner
but she gets everywhere first. She grows and grows till she's
as big as the room. And then I hear the door open but I can't
move, Christine. I can't breathe.

CHRISTINE. (*Rocking* LEA.) Hush. Hush now. It's over.
Try and sleep. Go to sleep.

LEA. I can't.

CHRISTINE. (*Sings.*)
Sleep my little sister, sleep
Sleep through darkness
Sleep so deep

LEA. You won't ever leave me, will you, Christine?

CHRISTINE. (*Sings.*)
All the rivers find the sea
My little sister
Sleep for me.

LEA. (*Touching* CHRISTINE'S *face.*) You won't, will you?

CHRISTINE. (*Holding* LEA *close.*) Never.

LEA. I don't think I could bear it—being alone in this
house. In any house. (MADAME DANZARD *appears at the
top of the stairs. She is wearing a bathrobe and slippers
and is carrying a kerosene lamp. She comes down the
stairs on tiptoe and goes into the dining room.*)

CHRISTINE. (*Sings.*)
Dream my little sister, dream
Dream I'm here now
Dream your dreams

LEA. Do you hear me, Christine?

CHRISTINE. (*Sings.*)
All the things you want to be
My little sister
Dream for me.

(*Softly,* MADAME DANZARD *moves across the floor to
the cabinet, opens it quietly, takes out a long black box, on
top of which lies the white glove, opens it, and silently be-*

gins counting the silverware.)

LEA. I was so scared when Madame was waiting when we came back from the square. Weren't you scared, Christine?

CHRISTINE. Madame doesn't speak to us anymore. She hasn't said a word in months.

LEA. She never did, Christine. Oh Christine, she never did.

CHRISTINE. Shhh. Sleep now. Sleep my angel. (*Continues the song.*)
Somewhere there are meadows
Somewhere there are hills
Somewhere horses run
And sheep are still
(MADAME DANZARD *closes the box, lays the white glove carefully on top, returns the box to the cabinet, picks up the kerosene lamp, and quietly goes up the staircase.*) (*Sings.*)
Sleep my little sister, sleep
Cows will moo
And lambs will bleat
I will never leave your side
My little sister
Close your eyes.
(*As the light dims,* LEA'S *eyes remain wide open, staring into the darkness.*)

SCENE 11

The sound of a 1930's song, "Chez Moi" is heard on the radio.* Light comes up on an empty house. A door fans open and shut to the music. ISABELLE

*"*Chez Moi*" (Venez Donc Chez Moi) Copyright © 1935. Fox-trot avec refrain chanté (P. Misraki — J. Feline)

dances out into the sitting room, carrying a hair-brush and an ivory mirror. In a 1930's pose, she brushes her hair and gazes at herself in the mirror. She puts the hairbrush and mirror down on the table, flings herself onto the couch and plucks an imaginary cigarette out of the air. She dances over to the staircase, tests the banister for imaginary dust. She goes quickly to the cabinet and takes out a chocolate. She throws the wrapper on the table and pops the chocolate into her mouth. CHRISTINE *comes down the hallway on her hands and knees, dusting the moulding of the staircase.* ISABELLE *puts on* MADAME DANZARD'S *hat, plunges in the hatpin, and dances over to the bottom of the stairs.* CHRISTINE *sees* ISABELLE *and stands up.* ISABELLE *stops dancing immediately. They stare at each other.* ISABELLE *turns off the radio. A soft drip of water begins.* CHRISTINE *starts polishing the banister.* ISABELLE *stands in the sitting room.* LEA *appears carrying a silver centerpiece. She puts it on the dining room table, not noticing* CHRISTINE *on the staircase.* ISABELLE *looks at* CHRISTINE. *She picks up the hairbrush and the mirror. She holds out the brush to* LEA. LEA *hesitates. Finally she takes the brush from* ISABELLE *and starts brushing her hair.* ISABELLE *smiles, luxuriating in* LEA'S *brushing her hair.* CHRISTINE *watches them.* MADAME DANZARD *appears at the top of the stairs. She sees* CHRISTINE *polishing the banister, the same spot over and over again.* CHRISTINE *sees* MADAME DANZARD, *stops, and goes into the kitchen. She begins to struggle with the cover of a canister. She cannot get it off.* MADAME DANZARD *comes all the way down the stairs and stands watching* LEA *brush* ISABELLE'S *hair.* ISABELLE *sees* MADAME DANZARD *and takes the hairbrush from* LEA.

She goes out. LEA, *finally seeing* MADAME DANZARD, *follows her.* ISABELLE *closes the door in* LEA'S *face.* LEA *comes back, stands still, nervously watching* MADAME DANZARD. MADAME DANZARD *takes the chocolate wrapper from the table and flicks it onto the floor. She looks at* LEA. *Confused,* LEA *doesn't move. Pinching* LEA'S *arm,* MADAME DANZARD *drags her over to where the chocolate wrapper has fallen. She pushes* LEA *down on her knees.* LEA *picks up the wrapper. There is a loud banging sound. In the kitchen,* CHRISTINE *is struggling desperately with the canister. She bangs it several times on the table.* MADAME DANZARD, *hearing the noise, goes into the kitchen. Seeing her,* CHRISTINE *places the canister carefully on the table. The sound of the drip grows louder.* MADAME DANZARD *checks a pot, opens the door of a cabinet and closes it. Holding the chocolate wrapper,* LEA *goes out the hall.* MADAME DANZARD *turns off the dripping faucet.* CHRISTINE *watches her.* MADAME DANZARD *looks at Christine, leaves the kitchen and goes down the hall. the light dims.*

SCENE 12

ISABELLE *stands on a stool in the middle of the sitting room. She is trying on a drab mauve dress, much too large on her.* CHRISTINE *is on her knees, pinning up the hem of the dress. Around her neck hangs a large pair of tailor scissors.* LEA *holds the pins and hands them to* CHRISTINE. MADAME DANZARD *stands looking up at* ISABELLE. *Throughout the scene,* CHRISTINE *makes adjustments on the dress—hem, sleeves, waist, bodice. Never, during any point in the scene, is a word addressed to* CHRISTINE *or* LEA.

MADAME DANZARD. What did I tell you? It's perfect.

ISABELLE. Yes Maman. (*After a pause.*) Do you really think so?

MADAME DANZARD. Of course I think so. You're always so difficult when it comes to clothes.

ISABELLE. I'm not difficult. (*Looking down at the dress.*) I just didn't like it.

MADAME DANZARD. Well you see — you were wrong. You really should trust me, Isabelle. Have I ever chosen anything you didn't like? (ISABELLE *is silent.*) Eventually?

ISABELLE. It looks better at home. (CHRISTINE *starts taking in the right sleeve of* ISABELLE'S *dress.*)

MADAME DANZARD. Of course it does. Everything always looks better at home. I want you to wear it Friday when we go to the Flintons'.

ISABELLE. But it won't be ready in —

MADAME DANZARD. (*Interrupting.*) It will be ready. She hardly has anything to do.

ISABELLE. Must we go, Maman? The Flintons are so —

MADAME DANZARD. We're going. And put your arm down, Isabelle. Remember how long she took the last time. (*She touches the bodice of the dress.*) You know my dear, I think it's too tight around the chest. (CHRISTINE *moves to* ISABELLE'S *right side and undoes the pins around her chest.*) Yes, I really think so. You don't want to wear these things too tight. Though they are wearing them tight these days. I saw Mademoiselle Loupin on the Rue Mafort just yesterday. I couldn't believe my eyes.

ISABELLE. Oh you can't count her. Everything looks tight around her chest. (CHRISTINE *moves behind* ISABELLE.)

MADAME DANZARD. (*Barely restraining a laugh.*)

Isabelle! How unlike you. I never even thought you'd noticed Mademoiselle Loupin.

ISABELLE. Of course I've noticed her. Who hasn't? (CHRISTINE *moves to* ISABELLE's *left side.*)

MADAME DANZARD. She's getting married in September Monsieur Bouttier told me at the pharmacy. The date is definitely set.

ISABELLE. (*Smiling.*) So they say.

MADAME DANZARD. Why—do you have any reason to doubt it?

ISABELLE. None.

MADAME DANZARD. You sounded so . . . Anyway I know one marriage that's going to take place. (*She smiles to herself.* CHRISTINE *trembles suddenly, holds the pins out to* LEA *who is not paying attention to her. The pins fall to the floor in front of the footstool.* CHRISTINE *and* LEA *bend down to pick up the pins.* CHRISTINE's *hands are shaking.* MADAME DANZARD *watches.*) Those first few months of being married, my dear. (*Looking at* CHRISTINE *and* LEA.) Some people will never know.

ISABELLE. (*Smiling.*) Maman. (LEA *looks up at* ISABELLE. CHRISTINE *stands up, and looks down at* LEA. LEA *moves to* CHRISTINE. ISABELLE *watches her.* MADAME DANZARD *and* CHRISTINE *look at each other.*)

MADAME DANZARD. (*Moving closer.*) Now how am I going to take you to the Flintons with a crooked hem? Hmmm? Just tell me that. (ISABELLE *tries to look down at the hem. Glaring at* CHRISTINE.) Don't move, Isabelle. Don't budge. (*Hastily,* CHRISTINE *starts redoing the hem. Watching her.*) Incredible how long it takes to do a simple hem. (CHRISTINE *continues to fix the hem.* MADAME DANZARD *suddenly moves in and rips the bottom of the dress out of* CHRISTINE's *hands. She points to the neck of the dress.*) The neck should be lower. Definitely lower. (CHRISTINE *takes the tailor scissors and slowly begins cutting away the fabric around the neck. Stepping forward.*) Impossible. (*She takes the scissors from* CHRISTINE, *with them gestures her away, and begins cutting the fabric around the neck herself.* CHRISTINE *starts up the stairs. Loudly, as she cuts.*) Really. And with crepe going for seven francs a yard. Next time we'll go to the dressmaker's. (*On the stairs,* CHRISTINE *stops. She continues up.* LEA *follows her.*) (*Taking a few steps back from* ISABELLE.) Your grandmother's pearls will look just right. You shall have them as a present.

ISABELLE. Maman! (*In their room,* CHRISTINE *sits down on the bed, facing out.* LEA *stands behind her.*)

MADAME DANZARD. I can already see you. And those pearls. A perfect match. (*The light dims slowly on* MADAME DANZARD *and* ISABELLE.)

CHRISTINE. There was nothing wrong with that hem. Nothing. You saw it. That hem was perfectly straight. (LEA *is silent.*) Wasn't it?

LEA. Of course it was.

CHRISTINE. She sees things. Things that aren't even there. Her and her daughter. (*She pauses.*) You won't go, will you?

LEA. Go where? Where would I go?

CHRISTINE. Even if she goes, you won't go. (LEA *is silent.*) Lea! You're thinking about it all the time, aren't you? That's why you're always dreaming. Why you're always off in that other world.

LEA. There is no other world, Christine. (*Coming closer.*) Christine—darling. Don't be upset.

CHRISTINE. You heard Madame. You heard what she said.

LEA. What did she say?

CHRISTINE. You heard her. Don't pretend you didn't.

LEA. I didn't hear anything.

CHRISTINE. Nothing about her daughter.

LEA. Mademoiselle Isabelle, you mean?

CHRISTINE. (*Turning on her.*) Who else?

LEA. (*Drawing back.*) Don't be like that, Christine. You sound just like Maman.

CHRISTINE. You smiled at her. I saw you.

LEA. I didn't smile—

CHRISTINE. (*Interrupting.*) She makes you do everything for her. You're always with her.

LEA. I—

CHRISTINE. (*Cutting in.*) Promise me you won't go. When she goes.

LEA. If she goes. She may never go. We've been over this a hundred times, Christine. She may never get marrie—

CHRISTINE. (*Overlapping.*) Answer me!

LEA. Christine.

CHRISTINE. (*Breaking in.*) Answer me! Don't just keep saying Christine. (*Anguished.*) Sometimes...every morning...I think of—I imagine—things...that you...

LEA. Christine.

CHRISTINE. You're all I have, little Lea. All I'll ever have. (*Holding* LEA.) Sometimes I think we'll never have enough time. Do you think we'll have enough time, Lea? The days seem to be getting longer. And the nights, ah Lea—the nights—(*Jumping up suddenly.*) There'll never be enough time for us. (*She starts pacing the room.*)

LEA. Come and sit with me.

CHRISTINE. In a minute.

LEA. When you walk like that it reminds me of Sister

Veronica. I used to hear her when I went to sleep. And when —

CHRISTINE. What?

LEA. She was angry when Maman took me away.

CHRISTINE. Angry?

LEA. I tried to talk to her. I followed her after morning mass. Remember the garden, Christine? Remember the path? (CHRISTINE *is silent, watching her.*) My shoes . . . my shoes kept clicking on the stone. I followed her all the way to her room. She was walking so fast her habit moved like a wind was blowing it. I got so close I almost tripped on it. But she wouldn't stop. She wouldn't turn around. She never turned around.

CHRISTINE. You never told me.

LEA. (*After a moment.*) Christine.

CHRISTINE. Yes?

LEA. I . . . um . . .

CHRISTINE. What is it?

LEA. (*Swallowing.*) I want you to. . .Would you. . .

CHRISTINE. What? (*Softly.*) Tell me. (*Watching her.*) Tell me.

LEA. Let's. . .Oh Christine, let's. . .let's pretend you're her.

CHRISTINE. Her?

LEA. Just be her.

CHRISTINE. Sister Veronica.

LEA. Yes.

CHRISTINE. I—(*Turning away. Smiling.*) Idiot!

LEA. Christine. Please.

CHRISTINE. Now?

LEA. Yes, now.

CHRISTINE. All right. (*Hesitating.*) Close your eyes. (LEA *closes her eyes.*)

LEA. Can I look yet?

CHRISTINE. Wait a second. (*She unties her long apron*

from around her waist.)

LEA. What are you doing?

CHRISTINE. Just a minute. You'll see. Don't be so impatient. (*She ties the apron around her head, so that it falls in front of her face, then slips it back so that it resembles a nun's habit.*) Now look.

LEA. You're ready?

CHRISTINE. (*Turning toward* LEA.) I'm ready. (LEA *opens her eyes, looks at* CHRISTINE. *The light dims.*)

SCENE 13

Sunday morning. Church bells are ringing. ISABELLE *is downstairs, ready to go out.*

ISABELLE. (*Picking up a calling card.*) Maman. Look! Madame Castelneuve was here.

MADAME DANZARD. (*Coming down the stairs.*) No!

ISABELLE. (*Picking up another calling card.*) And Madame Richepin.

MADAME DANZARD. How did they get in? When? The new curtains aren't even here yet. What's the matter with those two? They didn't even tell me. (*Irritated, tapping* ISABELLE *on the back.*) Don't slump, Isabelle. You know how I hate that. She asked me for another blanket yesterday.

ISABELLE. Incredible. Why should they complain about the cold? They're hardly ever in their room.

MADAME DANZARD. (*Taking two heavy prayer books, one for her, one for* ISABELLE.) No one in this town has a radiator in the maid's room. It's unheard of. Have you ever heard of such a thing?

ISABELLE. Never.

MADAME DANZARD. (*Putting on her gloves.*) They're in the kitchen from six in the morning till ten at night. They have the stove to keep them warm.

ISABELLE. You worry too much, Maman.

MADAME DANZARD. As if I don't make life easy for them in every way.

ISABELLE. You do everything for them. You're too good to them. (CHRISTINE *and* LEA *come running into the house, laughing. They are dressed in their identical coats and hats, and wear white gloves. They stop when they see* MADAME DANZARD *and* ISABELLE. *Quietly they go up the stairs into their room.*) Did you see them? Coming back from church.

MADAME DANZARD. Spotless—with their white gloves. They don't even look like maids anymore. (*Softly* LEA *closes the door. She laughs and whirls* CHRISTINE *around.* CHRISTINE *puts her hand over* LEA'S *mouth.* LEA *begins pulling off* CHRISTINE'S *gloves.*) But they're losing their looks, my dear. Have you noticed? Have you seen how thin they've become? Especially the younger one. (LEA *takes off* CHRISTINE'S *hat.* CHRISTINE *sits still, watching her.* LEA *smiles, takes a few steps back.*) And those circles under their eyes.

ISABELLE. They look like they never sleep. (LEA *takes off her gloves. She turns and looks at* CHRISTINE.) (*Suddenly touching the banister.*) Look at this, Maman.

MADAME DANZARD. At what?

ISABELLE. Don't you see? (*Pointing.*) There. Right there.

MADAME DANZARD. (*Turning back.*) What is it? (ISABELLE *points again. Looking carefully.*) Oh yes. I see. Yes. They're getting careless. (LEA *takes off her hat. The* DANZARDS *go out. The heavy front door slams.* LEA *undoes her hair. It falls around her. Slowly, she unbuttons her coat, pulls it open. She is wearing the elaborate white chemise with the wide shoulder straps*

CHRISTINE *sewed for her.* LEA *begins to move around the room. Her movements have a strange grace of their own. She moves all over the small room, her hair flying.* CHRISTINE *watches her. Suddenly, she pulls* LEA *down to her. The light dims.*)

SCENE 14

The sound of water dripping. Slowly CHRISTINE *comes down the stairs. She goes into the kitchen and turns off the faucet. From the cabinet she takes a tray and places it on the kitchen table. From the sink she takes four drying wine glasses. She polishes them, places them on the tray. The fourth glass breaks in her hand. She draws her cut hand to her mouth, licking away the blood. She wraps her hand in a napkin. With the other hand, she puts the broken pieces of glass in the sink. She takes the tray with the polished wine glasses to the cabinet. Upstairs, in their room, the lights go out.*

LEA. (*Voice over. Screaming.*) Christine!

CHRISTINE. (*Almost dropping the tray.*) What is it?

LEA. (*Screaming.*) Oh no, no! Christine!

CHRISTINE. (*Running to the bottom of the stairs.*) What is it? What happened? (LEA *comes down the stairs to the landing.*)

LEA. The iron. It blew the fuse.

CHRISTINE. Oh no.

LEA. What will Madame do to us? What will she do? (CHRISTINE *goes to the kitchen cabinet and takes out a candle and matches.* LEA *comes down the stairs.*) I was right in the middle of her satin blouse.

CHRISTINE. (*Whirling around, the candle in her hand.*) Did you burn it?

LEA. It's the second time something's gone wrong with that iron.

CHRISTINE. Answer me, Lea. Did you?

LEA. First Mademoiselle's dress and now—

CHRISTINE. Did you burn it?

LEA. Madame will be so angry. Madame will be furious.

CHRISTINE. How can Madame be angry? It's not your fault. She can't be angry. (*She starts up the stairs with the candle.*) Let me see the blouse. (LEA *grabs at her arm.*) Let me see it. (*She goes up the stairs.*)

LEA. (*Frozen on the staircase.*) Is it all right?

CHRISTINE. (*Voice over.*) Just a minute.

LEA. (*Nervous.*) Is it? (*Panicked, running up the stairs.*) Is it? (CHRISTINE *comes into their room, spent.* LEA *comes in after her.*)

CHRISTINE. Don't worry.

LEA. Are you sure?

CHRISTINE. It's all right, Lea.

LEA. (*Sitting down on the bed.*) I'm so tired. That was the last thing left. And what will happen now, Christine? What will happen now?

CHRISTINE. Nothing will happen. There's nothing we can do. Don't worry, Lea. They've gone to the Blanchards for dinner. They'll play cards all night. We just have to wait.

LEA. Christine—how much money do we have saved?

CHRISTINE. Not enough.

LEA. I know it's not enough. But it will be one day. (CHRISTINE *is silent.*) It will be, won't it?

CHRISTINE. Hush, hush. Rest. Rest now.

LEA. And then —then we'll go away from here and — (CHRISTINE *is still.*) And—

CHRISTINE. (*Quietly.*) Yes. Yes my Lea. (*She begins to undo* LEA'S *long braid.*) Someday. (*There is a pause.*)

LEA. (*Devastated, beginning to cry.*) I burned it, didn't I? Didn't I? Tell me.

CHRISTINE. My angel. My love. It's all right. (CHRISTINE *puts her arms around* LEA. *On the bed they undo each other's hair. There is the sound of hairpins falling on the floor. There is a pause. The sound of a key turning in a lock.* MADAME DANZARD *and* ISABELLE *enter downstairs. They are carrying several small packages tied with string. In one hand,* MADAME DANZARD *holds a set of heavy keys.*) DANZARD *holds a set of neavy keys.*)

MADAME DANZARD. (*Impatient.*) Where is she?

ISABELLE. How do I know?

MADAME DANZARD. Don't answer me like that. Go and find her. (ISABELLE *doesn't move. There is something ominous about the house.*) (*Putting down her package and gloves.*) Did you hear what I said? This is absurd. She should be here to take these packages. She should have been here to open the door. At five thirty in the afternoon — what time is it anyway?

ISABELLE. (*Looking at her watch.*) Five forty-five.

MADAME DANZARD. (*Looking at her watch.*) Five forty-five. I mean really. Five forty-five and not a sign of them. I never heard of anything like it. Go into the kitchen, Isabelle. They must be there. (ISABELLE *goes into the kitchen. On the bed upstairs,* LEA *and* CHRISTINE *are in shadow.* ISABELLE *finds the broken glass and a dish in the sink.*)

CHRISTINE. (*Sitting up.*) Lea! Listen. (LEA *sits up.* ISABELLE *comes back from the kitchen.*)

MADAME DANZARD. Well? What took you so long?

CHRISTINE. It's them.

LEA. (*Her eyes wide with terror.*) Oh no.

ISABELLE. They're not there, Maman. And — (LEA *and* CHRISTINE *sit huddled together.*)

MADAME DANZARD. Impossible. *I'll* look. They must be there... And what?

ISABELLE. There's a dish in there... And a glass. Broken.

MADAME DANZARD. (*Going to the kitchen and picking up the broken glass in the sink.*) Broken. Nerve. What can they be doing?

LEA. Maybe they'll go away.

MADAME DANZARD. (*Listening.*) Shhh. Listen.

CHRISTINE. Shhh.

MADAME DANZARD. (*Looking out into the audience.*) Maybe they're upstairs.

LEA. What will we do, Christine?

CHRISTINE. Lea.

LEA. What will we do?

CHRISTINE. Little Lea. Wait, let me think.

MADAME DANZARD. I'm going up there this minute. (CHRISTINE *stands up.*)

CHRISTINE. I have to go down.

ISABELLE. Maman—wait.

LEA. Wait.

MADAME DANZARD. Wait? What for?

CHRISTINE. Do you want them to come up here?

ISABELLE. I don't think you should.

MADAME DANZARD. This is my house. Of course I'm going upstairs. Right now. (*She starts up the stairs.*)

CHRISTINE. If I don't go down, they'll come up.

MADAME DANZARD. You don't have to come if you don't want to. (ISABELLE *follows her slowly.*)

LEA. I'm frightened, Christine. I'm frightened. (MADAME DANZARD *stops.*)

MADAME DANZARD. (*Looking up.*) What's this? The lights are off up here. (CHRISTINE *leaves.*)

LEA. (*Terrorized.*) Don't leave me!

MADAME DANZARD. (*Quietly but furiously.*) This is really something. (*She and* ISABELLE *start down the staircase.* CHRISTINE *appears at the top of the stairs, her hair loose for the first time.*)

CHRISTINE. Madame. (ISABELLE *lets out a little shriek.*) Madame has come back.

MADAME DANZARD. What is this? How dare you expect me to come back to a dark house?

CHRISTINE. (*Coming down the stairs, putting her right foot first on each step.*) It was the iron, Madame.

MADAME DANZARD. *Again?* Unbelieveable. That's the second time. That iron was just repaired. What about my satin blouse?

ISABELLE. She came back to change into it.

MADAME DANZARD. Your sister didn't burn it, did she? She didn't burn my blouse?

CHRISTINE. Madame's blouse isn't finished yet.

MADAME DANZARD. (*Interrupting.*) Not finished? I'm wearing it to the Blanchards. What's the matter with your sister? (CHRISTINE *is silent.*) And why weren't you downstairs? Where's your apron?

CHRISTINE. (*Covering her uniform with her hands.*) I finished early, Madame.

ISABELLE. There's a dish in there. A glass. Broken.

MADAME DANZARD. Don't lie to me. I won't have a liar in this house.

CHRISTINE. Madame knows I don't lie.

ISABELLE. She is lying. I can tell.

MADAME DANZARD. You disappoint me. Send your sister down with my satin blouse at once. (CHRISTINE *doesn't move.*) Did you hear me? Go.

CHRISTINE. Madame can't see my sister now.

MADAME DANZARD. What?

ISABELLE. Are you going to let her speak to you like that?

MADAME DANZARD. I will see your sister this instant.

And she will explain how she ruined my iron for the second time.

CHRISTINE. I already explained to Madame about the iron.

MADAME DANZARD. You call that an explanation?

CHRISTINE. It wasn't our fault, Madame.

MADAME DANZARD. Not your fault? No? Whose fault was it then? (*She turns to* ISABELLE.) Did you hear that?

ISABELLE. I heard. Who knows what else they've done.

CHRISTINE. We haven't done anything.

MADAME DANZARD. How dare you? How dare you speak to my daughter like that?

CHRISTINE. If Madame can't trust us, if she suspects anything —

MADAME DANZARD. (*Interrupting.*) Suspect what?

CHRISTINE. (*Quickly.*) We'll leave this house.

MADAME DANZARD. You'll leave? And just where do you think you'll go?

CHRISTINE. We'll find another house. (MADAME DANZARD, *clenching her fists, is silent for a moment.*)

MADAME DANZARD. Will you? Not with the recommendation you get from me. Don't think you'll get out so easily. Not after what I've seen tonight.

CHRISTINE. (*Breaking in.*) Madame has seen nothing.

MADAME DANZARD. Nothing? (*Snorting.*) That face, that hair. You smell of it, my dear.

CHRISTINE. Madame, stop. Madame. Please.

MADAME DANZARD. (*Pushing* CHRISTINE *down and going up to the landing.*) Not another word out of your mouth. Breaking my iron. The house in darkness.

CHRISTINE. (*Looking up at her.*) I told Madame. It wasn't our fault.

MADAME DANZARD. (*Looking down at* CHRISTINE,

starting to yell.) Going to church every Sunday. Thinking you were a child of God. (*Raging, crossing herself.*) Forgive me God for what I have harboured here.

CHRISTINE. Madame. You have no right. (LEA *leaves their room.*)

MADAME DANZARD. (*Shrieking.*) No right? You must be mad.

ISABELLE. She is mad. Just look at her.

MADAME DANZARD. *You* have no rights, Christine. (LEA *appears at the top of the stairs.* ISABELLE *gasps.*)

ISABELLE. (*Grabbing her mother's arm.*) Maman! (CHRISTINE *runs up the stairs to* LEA.)

MADAME DANZARD. Look at that sister of yours. Dirt. (*She spits at them.*) Scum. Scum sisters. (*Her face twitching,* CHRISTINE *holds onto* LEA.)

CHRISTINE. (*Continuously.*) Not my sister, not my sister. (*She steps forward.* LEA *comes down the stairs.*)

MADAME DANZARD. You'll never work with your sister again.

ISABELLE. (*Trying to push past her mother.*) No one will take you. (LEA *tries to push past* CHRISTINE *toward* ISABELLE.)

CHRISTINE. (*Overlapping.*) Not my sister, not my sister.

LEA. (*Lifting the pewter pitcher high above* ISABELLE's *head.*) CHRISTINE! (*At the same moment, in a violent gesture,* CHRISTINE *leaps toward* MADAME DANZARD's *face. Blackout.*)

CHRISTINE. NOT MY SISTER!

ISABELLE. (*Overlapping.*) MAMAN! (MADAME DANZARD *screams wildly. Certain gestures may be made clear, others not. In the darkness are sounds of footsteps, screams, the thump of pewter on flesh. The screams gradually turn into moans in the quiet black house.*)

SCENE 15

Light comes up on CHRISTINE *and* LEA, *standing separately.*

MEDICAL EXAMINER. (*Voice over. A flat anonymous voice.*) On the last step of the staircase, a single eye was found, intact, complete with the optic nerve. The eye had been torn out without the aid of an instrument. (*He pauses.*) The bodies of Madame and Mademoiselle Danzard were found on the landing. On the ground were fragments of bone and teeth, a yellow diamond earring, two eyes, hair pins, a pocketbook, a set of keys, a coat button. The walls and doors were covered with splashes of blood reaching a height of seven feet.

JUDGE. (*Voice over.*) Is this the pewter pitcher with which you struck them down? (LEA *looks up.*)

MEDICAL EXAMINER. (*Voice over.*) Madame Danzard's body lay face up, Mademoiselle Danzard's body face down, the coat pulled up, the skirt pulled up, the underpants pulled down, revealing deep wounds on the buttocks and multiple slashes on the calves. Madame Danzard's eyes had been torn out of their sockets.

JUDGE. (*Voice over.*) The carving knife with which you slashed them? (CHRISTINE *looks up. They are silent.*) What did you have against Madame and Mademoiselle Danzard? (*He pauses.*) Was Madame good to you? (*He pauses.*) Did anything abnormal happen between you and your sister? (*He pauses.*) You understand me, don't you? Was it simply sisterly love? (*He pauses.*) How did you tear out their eyes? With your fingers? (CHRISTINE *clasps herself and rocks back and forth.*) Speak! You are here to defend yourselves.

You will be judged.

CHRISTINE. Lea. I want Lea. Please. I beg you. Forgive me. I'll be good. I promise. I won't cry anymore. Give me Lea. Give me my sister. (*With a terrible, long drawn out cry.*) LEA! (LEA *moves to the center. Her face is pale, her eyes vacant.*)

JUDGE. (*Voice over.*) Lea Lutton. You will perform ten years of hard labor. You are refused the right to enter the town of Le Mans for twenty years. (*He pauses.* CHRISTINE *stands beside* LEA.) Christine Lutton. You will be taken barefoot, wearing a chemise, your head covered by a black veil, to a public place in the town of Le Mans. And there, before your fellow citizens, your head will be severed from your body.

LEA. (*Gazing straight out, sings brokenly.*)
Sleep my little sister, sleep
Sleep through darkness
Sleep so deep
All the rivers find the sea
My little sister
Sleep for me.

(CHRISTINE *looks directly out.* LEA *gazes vaguely into the distance. They stand as if framed in a photograph.*)

THE END OF THE PLAY

COSTUME LIST

CHRISTINE —
Scene 1:
Brown dress with
    white collar
Short apron
Black stockings
Dark brown shoes

Scene 2:
Add: brown coat

Scene 3:
Nightgown
Chemise
Stockings
Add: maid's uniform
Long apron
Shoes

Scene 4:
Same

Scene 5:
Same

Scene 6:
Plain brown dress
Coat

Scene 8:
Uniform
Long apron

Scene 9:
Dark blue dress with
    wide lace collar
Dark blue coat

Scene 10:
Uniform
Long apron

Scene 11:
Nightgown

Scene 12:
Uniform
Long apron

Scene 13:
Same

Scene 14:
Add: coat
Beret
Pr. of white gloves

Scene 15:
Add: long apron

Scene 16:
Remove: apron

LEA—Scene 1:
Blue and black plaid
  smock
Black stockings
Bloomers
Black shoes

Scene 2:
Carry: brown sweater
  coat

Scene 3:
Plain chemise
Nightgown
Add: maid's uniform
Apron
Shoes

Scene 4:
Same

Scene 5:
Same

Scene 6:
Smock
Sweater coat

Scene 7:
Remove: plain chemise
Add: elaborate chemise
  with wide shoulder straps

Scene 8:
Uniform
Apron

Scene 9:
Dark blue dress with
  wide lace collar
Dark blue coat

Scene 10:
Uniform
Apron
Pink sweater

Scene 11:
Nightgown

Scene 12:
Uniform
Apron

Scene 13:
Same

Scene 14:
Elaborate chemise
Dark coat
Beret
Pr. of white gloves

Scene 15:
Uniform

Scene 16:
Same

MADAME DANZARD —
Scene 2:
White blouse
Brown skirt
Gray sweater
Stockings
Brown shoes
Wrist watch
Wedding ring
Brooch
Pearl earrings
Handkerchief

Scene 4:
Same

Scene 5:
Same

Scene 7:
Add: brown coat
Black hat w/hat pin
Pr. of gray gloves
Brown handbag

Scene 8:
Remove: coat, hat
Carry: hat, jacket

Scene 10:
Two-piece green suit
Blouse
Pearl necklace

Scene 11:
Bathrobe
Slippers
Hairnet

Scene 12:
Green suit

Scene 13:
Same

Scene 14:
Add: brown coat
Hat
Brown gloves
Brown scarf

Scene 15:
Remove: brown scarf
Add: black scarf

Isabelle—
Scene 2:
White short-sleeved blouse
Plaid jumper
Stockings
Brown shoes
String tie
Wrist watch
Barrettes

Scene 4:
Same

Scene 5:
Same

Scene 7:
Add: coat
Hat with feathers
Brown handbag

Scene 8:
Remove: coat, hat, bag

Scene 10:
Long sleeved blouse
Two piece striped dress
Thin belt
Barrettes

Scene12:
Same

Scene 13:
Remove: blouse, dress
Add: mauve dress
    with straight pins

Scene 14:
Remove: mauve dress
Add: blouse, striped dress,
    coat, felt hat, brown
    handbag, white gloves

Scene 15:
Remove: gloves
Add: tan knit gloves,
    beige scarf

FURNITURE AND PROPERTY PLOT

Preshow Preset

Onstage:

Kitchen —
Icebox
On top: candle in holder, box of kitchen matches, small bowl of water
Slop bucket with metal lid next to icebox
Cabinet on wall
Inside: assorted plates, glasses
Work table
On it: silver serving tray with doily
On tray: platter of cut bread, carrots, condensed mushroom soup (veal)
Fork
2 pieces of cheese on a plate
1 high wooden stool with upholstered seat
1 low metal stool
1 stove
On rear right warmer: iron skillet
On front right burner: covered iron pot
1 sink
In it: 3 wine glasses, 1 breakaway wine glass, 1 small plate, 1 collander with 1 1/2 lbs. of green beans
On counter: white enamel bowl
On faucets: wash rag
On edge of sink: damp cloth
1 folded dishtowel between sink and stove

Staircase —
Small rectangular rug
1 small silver plate for mail in niche
1 tan suitcase

72

In it: maid's uniform (Christine), apron (Christine)
alarm clock, towel, hairbrush
1 brown suitcase
In it: maid's uniform (Lea), apron (Lea), crocheted
blanket preset with loose strand of yarn

Dining Room —
1 table
On it:
1 large white tablecloth
1 small white cloth overlay
2 plates (2 small pieces of cut bread (paté) on Isabelle's
plate)
2 forks
2 knives
2 wine glasses — 1/2 full white grape juice
1 small loaf of bread
1 pot of butter
1 small hand bell
2 matching side chairs
1 secretary
In desk: photo albun with 1 loose photo, wooden box
with loose silver spoons
On lower shelf: 1 right hand white glove
On middle shelf: 1 prayer book

Sitting Room —
1 footstool
On it: sewing bag
In it: embroidery on a hoop, needle, thread, seed pearl
bag with handkerchief inside, needle, thread, box of
loose seed pearls and thimble
1 settee
1 low table in front of settee

On it: manicure set
1 bottle of pink nail polish
1 bottle of clear nail polish
1 glass bowl of cotton balls
1 glass dish filled with prunes (chocolates) wrapped in gold foil
1 console
On it: 1 radio with practical speaker inside
1 hankerchief (Madame Danzard)

Bedroom—
1 single iron bed
On it: 1 sheet, 1 pillow in case, 1 bedspread
Under it: 1 small hinged trunk filled with lingerie
1 sink
In it: small bowl of water
1 small mirror on pillar

Outside Front Door—
1 letter in blue envelope (Lea)
1 letter in white envelope (Madame Danzard)

Offstage:

Stage Right:
apron with needle & thread (Lea)
fancy chemise (Christine)
metal cannister (Christine)
mortar & pestle with cracker crumbs (Christine)
dough board with ball of dough (Christine)
pr. of sewing scissors on a ribbon (Christine)
pewter pitcher with bunch of dried flowers (Christine)

Center:
assorted rags
brass candlestick and polishing cloth (Christine)
candle in holder with glass chimney (Madame Danzard)
box matches
school bell
prayer book (Isabelle)
calling cards (Isabelle)
1 wine hand bag (Isabelle)
1 rust soft hat (Isabelle)
1 black hand bag with large keys in it (Madame Danzard)
1 pr. of tan gloves (Isabelle)
1 black hat with hat pin in it (Madame Danzard)
1 brown hat with feathers and trim (Isabelle)
1 silver centerpiece (Lea)
2 lace doilies (Lea)

Stage Left:
1 pillow with cloth over it (Isabelle)
1 hairbrush and hand mirror (Isabelle)
1 box with 2 decks of playing cards (see CARD PLOT)
1 silver dish with white after dinner mints (bouche)
1 small handbag (Isabelle)
1 large brown package tied with string (Isabelle)
1 medium white package tied with string (Madame Danzard)
1 black scarf (Madame Danzard)
1 tan scarf with brown stripe (Isabelle)
1 pr. of tan wool gloves (Isabelle)
1 framed photograph wrapped in paper (Madame Danzard)

DECK #1: MADAME DANZARD

Working from bottom to the top with the cards face down the pile should be arranged in this sequence:

A(H), 4(D), J(H), 9(C), 10(D), 8(D), 4(S), 8(S), 6(H), 7(S), 2(H), K(H), 9(H), J(S), 10(S), 3(D), 3(H), K(D), 3(C), 7(D), 5(C), J(D), Q(S), 2(D), 2(C), 6(D), K(C), J(C), Q(C), 4(C), A(D), 5(D), 7(H), 10(H), 3(S), 7(C), 8(C), 4(H), K(S), 6(C), A(S), 9(S), 5(H), Q(H), Q(D), 10(C), 5(S), 2(S), 6(S), A(C), 9(D)

ROW (Pile)	1	2	3	4	5	6	7
							Q(D)
						10(C)	4(H)
					5(S)	K(S)	5(D)
				2(S)	6(C)	7(H)	2(C)
Face-Down			6(S)	A(S)	10(H)	6(D)	K(D)
Cards:		A(C)	9(S)	3(S)	K(C)	3(C)	2(H)
Face-Up Cards:	9(D)	5(H)	7(C)	J(C)	7(D)	K(H)	9(C)
	Q(H)	8(C)	Q(C)	5(C)	9(H)	10(D)	
	8(H)	4(C)	J(D)	J(S)	8(D)		
	A(D)	Q(S)	10(S)	4(S)			
	2(D)	3(D)	8(S)				
	3(H)	6(H)					
	7(S)						

Stock Cards: J(H)
4(D)
A(H)

DECK #2: ISABELLE

Sequence:

J(C), 4(D), Q(H), 10(C), K(D), 9(H), 6(C),
3(S), 7(S), 10(D), 8(D), 9(S), K(C), 8(S),
Q(S), Q(C), 7(C), 7(D), 2(D), 5(S), A(C),
6(D), 9(D), 9(C), K(S), 5(H), 6(S), 2(C),
Q(D), 3(C), J(S), 4(C), 6(H), 4(H), 8(C),
3(H), 7(H), J(H), 10(S), J(D), 5(C), 2(H),
10(H), A(S), A(H), 8(H), 5(D), 4(S), K(H),
3(D), 2(S), A(D).

ROW (Pile)	1	2	3	4	5	6	7
							8(H)
						5(D)	10(S)
					4(S)	J(D)	4(C)
				K(H)	5(C)	6(H)	A(D)
			3(D)	2(H)	4(H)	5(H)	7(D)
		2(S)	10(H)	8(C)	6(S)	2(D)	8(D)
Face-Up Cards:	A(D)	A(S)	3(H)	2(C)	5(S)	9(S)	10(C)
	A(H)	7(H)	Q(D)	A(C)	K(C)	K(D)	
	J(H)	3(C)	6(D)	8(S)	9(H)		
	J(S)	9(D)	Q(S)	6(C)			
	9(C)	Q(C)	3(S)				
	7(C)	7(S)					
	10(D)						

Stock Cards: Q(H)
4(D)
J(C)

CARD PLOT

MADAME DANZARD: ". . . Just a minute   (page 41)
now."
   MADAME DANZARD moves seven of clubs
(pile #3) to eight of diamonds (pile #5). SHE
turns over nine of spades (pile #3).

MADAME DANZARD: ". . . things a little
easier."   (page 41)
   ISABELLE moves queen of spades (pile #3)
to king of diamonds (pile #6).

ISABELLE: "I see it, Maman."   (page 41)
   ISABELLE moves six of diamonds (pile #3)
to seven of spades (pile #2).

MADAME DANZARD: "The nine of   (page 41)
diamonds onto the ten of clubs."
   ISABELLE moves nine of diamonds (pile #2)
to ten of clubs (pile #7).

MADAME DANZARD: "Red eight on black   (page 41)
nine on red ten . . ."
   MADAME DANZARD moves eight of hearts
(pile #1) to nine of clubs (pile #7).

MADAME DANZARD: "Perfect!"   (page 41)
   MADAME DANZARD turns over two of
hearts (pile #7).

MADAME DANZARD: ". . . all these with   (page 41)
the jack . . ."
   MADAME DANZARD moves jack of clubs
(pile #4) to queen of hearts (pile #1).

MADAME DANZARD: "What's been hiding   (page 41)
from me."
   MADAME DANZARD turns up three of
spades (pile #4).
   ISABELLE moves eight of spades (pile #4) to

nine of hearts (pile #5). SHE puts up ace of
clubs (pile #4).   (page 41)
ISABELLE: "I've got it, Maman."
  ISABELLE puts up two of clubs (pile #4).   (page 41)
ISABELLE: "And the three."
  ISABELLE puts up three of clubs (pile #2).
  SHE turns up eight of clubs (pile #4).   (page 42)
MADAME DANZARD: "Where is the ace of
diamonds?"
  ISABELLE moves seven of hearts (pile #2) to
  eight of clubs (pile #4).   (page 42)
ISABELLE: "But I've got the ace of spades.
And the two . . ."
  ISABELLE puts up the ace of spades (pile
  #2) and the two of spades (pile #2).   (page 42)
ISABELLE: "Three!"
  ISABELLE puts up the three of spades
  (pile #3).   (page 42)
MADAME DANZARD: "Ah—there's the
four."
  MADAME DANZARD puts up the four of
  spades (pile #1).   (page 42)
ISABELLE: "I have the five."
  ISABELLE puts up the five of spades
  (pile #5).   (page 42)
ISABELLE: "And the six!"
  ISABELLE puts up the six of spades (pile
  #5). SHE turns over four of hearts.   (page 42)
MADAME DANZARD: "Seven, eight!"
  MADAME DANZARD puts up seven of
  spades (pile #6) and eight of spades (pile #7).   (page 42)
MADAME DANZARD: "And the nine, ten,
jack!"
  MADAME DANZARD puts up the nine of

spades (pile #4), ten of spades (pile #6), and
jack of spades (pile #1).

ISABELLE: "The queen!"   (page 43)
   ISABELLE puts up the queen of spades
   (pile #6).

MADAME DANZARD: "Have you turned up   (page 43)
your three cards yet?"
   ISABELLE moves jack of hearts (pile #1) to
   queen of diamonds (pile #3). This move frees
   ace of hearts (pile #1).

MADAME DANZARD: "Of course they're so   (page 43)
blind . . ."
   ISABELLE puts up ace of hearts without
   announcing this move to MADAME
   DANZARD.

ISABELLE: "I wasn't smiling, Maman."   (page 43)
   ISABELLE moves eight of clubs (pile #4) to
   nine of hearts (pile #5). SHE turns over two
   of hearts (pile #4).

MADAME DANZARD: "My two, my three."   (page 43)
   MADAME DANZARD puts up two of
   hearts (pile #7) and three of hearts (pile #4).

ISABELLE: "Here Maman. I have it."   (page 43)
   ISABELLE puts of four hearts (pile #5).

MADAME DANZARD: "It's finally come to   (page 44)
that."
   MADAME DANZARD turns over jack of
   hearts from her stock.

MADAME DANZARD: "But they knew."   (page 44)
   MADAME DANZARD turns over four of
   diamonds from her stock.

ISABELLE: "Take a chance."   (page 44)
   MADAME DANZARD turns over ace of
   hearts from her stock. SHE puts card up.

ISABELLE: "My ace, my two, my—"   (page 44)
   ISABELLE puts up ace of diamonds
   (pile #1) and two of diamonds (pile #6).
NOTE: From this point on to the end of the
   game both players made moves with cards
   without respect to color, suit, rank, etc.

   If preferred, the card game can be played by pretending to follow the order of the cards specified in the
   scene.

MY SISTER IN THIS HOUSE

"Sleep My Little Sister, Sleep"*

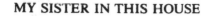

"Sleep My Little Sister, Sleep" page two

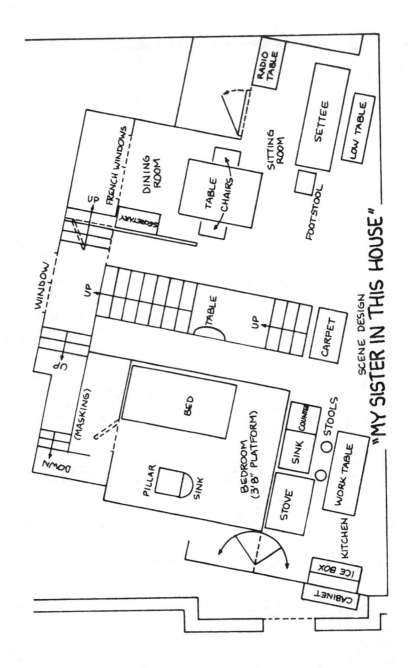

SCENE DESIGN
"MY SISTER IN THIS HOUSE"

Also By

Wendy Kesselman

DIARY OF ANNE FRANK (ADAPTATION)
I LOVE YOU, I LOVE YOU NOT
THE JUNIPER TREE, A TRAGIC HOUSEHOLD TALE
MAGGIE MAGALITA
MY SISTER IN THIS HOUSE

A PIECE OF MY HEART
Shirley Lauro

Drama / 1 m, 6 f / Unit set

This is a powerful, true drama of six women who went to Vietnam: five nurses and a country western singer booked by an unscrupulous agent to entertain the troops. The play portrays each young woman before, during and after her tour in the war-torn jungle and ends as each leaves a personal token at The Wall in Washington.

A Piece of My Heart premiered in New York at Manhattan Theatre Club, and now has enjoyed over 1000 productions there and abroad. It has also been named "The most enduring play on Vietnam in the nation," by The Vietnam Vets Association.

"There have been a number of plays dealing with Vietnam, but none with the direct, emotional impact of Ms. Lauro's work."
– *New York Times*

"Brought [the audience] to tears... and a standing ovation."
– *Variety*

OTHER TITLES AVAILABLE FROM SAMUEL FRENCH

THE RIVERS AND RAVINES
Heather McDonald

Drama / 9m, 5f / Unit Set
Originally produced to acclaim by Washington D.C.'s famed
Arena Stage. This is an engrossing political drama about the
contemporary farm crisis in America and its effect on rural
communities.

"A haunting and emotionally draining play. A community of
farmers and ranchers in a small Colorado town disintegrates
under the weight of failure and thwarted ambitions. Most of
the farmers, their spouses, children, clergyman, banker and
greasy spoon proprietress survive, but it is survival without
triumph. This is an *Our Town* for the 80's."
– *The Washington Post*

OTHER TITLES AVAILABLE FROM SAMUEL FRENCH

THREE YEARS FROM "THIRTY"
Mike O'Malley

Comic Drama / 4m, 3f / Unit set

This funny, poignant story of a group of 27-year-olds who have known each other since college sold out during its limited run at New York City's Sanford Meisner Theater. Jessica Titus, a frustrated actress living in Boston, has become distraught over local job opportunities and she is feeling trapped in her long standing relationship with her boyfriend Tom. She suddenly decides to pursue her dreams in New York City. Unbeknownst to her, Tom plans to propose on the evening she has chosen to leave him. The ensuing conflict ripples through their lives and the lives of their roommates and friends, leaving all of them to reconsider their careers, the paths of their souls and the questions, demands and definition of commitment.

OTHER TITLES AVAILABLE FROM SAMUEL FRENCH

MURDER AMONG FRIENDS
Bob Barry

Comedy thriller / 4m, 2f / Interior

Take an aging, exceedingly vain actor; his very rich wife; a double dealing, double loving agent, plunk them down in an elegant New York duplex and add dialogue crackling with wit and laughs, and you have the basic elements for an evening of pure, sophisticated entertainment. Angela, the wife and Ted, the agent, are lovers and plan to murder Palmer, the actor, during a contrived robbery on New Year's Eve. But actor and agent are also lovers and have an identical plan to do in the wife. A murder occurs, but not one of the planned ones.

"Clever, amusing, and very surprising."
– *New York Times*

"A slick, sophisticated show that is modern and very funny."
– WABC TV